Soups

A Pyramid Cookery Paperback

Soups

hamlyn

An Hachette Livre UK Company
www.hachettelivre.co.uk

A Pyramid Paperback

First published in Great Britain in 2004 by
Hamlyn, a division of Octopus Publishing Group Ltd,
2–4 Heron Quays, London E14 4JP
www.octopusbooksusa.com

This edition published 2009

Copyright © Octopus Publishing Group Ltd 2004, 2008

Distributed in the U.S. and Canada by Octopus
Books USA:
c/o Hachette Book Group USA
237 Park Avenue
New York NY 10017

ISBN 978-0-600-61955-0

A CIP catalog record for this book is available from the
British Library

Printed and bound in China

10 9 8 7 6 5 4 3 2 1

Notes

Ovens should be preheated to the specified
temperature. If using a fan-assisted oven, follow
the manufacturer's directions for adjusting the
time and temperature. Broilers should also be
preheated.

This book includes dishes made with nuts and nut
derivatives. It is advisable for those with known
allergic reactions to nuts and nut derivatives and
those who may be potentially vulnerable to these
allergies, such as pregnant and nursing mothers,
invalids, the elderly, babies, and children, to
avoid dishes made with nuts and nut oils. It is
also prudent to check the labels of preprepared
ingredients for the possible inclusion of nut
derivatives.

Fresh herbs should be used unless otherwise
stated. If unavailable use dried herbs as an
alternative but halve the quantities stated.

Contents

Introduction

Piping hot, cool and chilled, light and healthy, hearty and nutritious, rich and creamy, or sumptuous and sophisticated—soup comes in a thousand different forms. But there's one thing that every bowl of soup has in common—it's always a treat. Whether you're looking for the perfect comfort food or the ultimate health-kick, you will always find it in a bowl of soup.

A quick history

Soup has been eaten for millennia, ever since early man first discovered how to make vessels in which to boil food. The earliest soups were probably a by-product of cooking other foods in liquid—but as nothing was wasted in those times, the cooking broth was eaten too.

Today, every nation has its own soups—*sup, zuppe, shorba, sopa, pho* to name but a few. In Greece they eat egg and lemon *Avgolemono*. In Southeast Asia they enjoy fiery, fragrant broths, and creamy concoctions made with coconut milk. In Morocco the national soup is *Harira*, made of beans and lentils, which is favored during the month-long fast of Ramadan. In Russia it is *Borscht*—served chunky or smooth, hot or cold, but always a vibrant purplish-red.

Classic soups are constantly evolving, being re-invented each time different cultures and cuisines collide. *Mulligatawny* was adopted and adapted by the British stationed in India during colonial times, while many Vietnamese soups show a distinct French influence. Modern chefs love to take old recipes such as Venetian *Risi e* *Bisi* and Hungarian *Goulash* and transform them into new and utterly delicious soups.

Getting started

Soups are one of the easiest dishes to make and all the recipes in this book are simple to prepare and cook. All you need is a cutting board and knife, a large pot for cooking, and a wooden spoon for stirring. If the soup needs to be blended, a blender or food processor is invaluable. However, many soups can be pureed using a mouli or food mill, and coarse-textured vegetable soups can often be achieved simply by using a potato masher.

Perfect results

The key to a good soup is using good-quality ingredients, and the most important ingredient of all is stock. Stock forms the base of almost every soup, and it is upon this that all the other flavors build. A poor-quality stock can spoil a soup, no matter how delicious the other ingredients are. It is best to use fresh, homemade stock (see recipes on pages 8–11). However, you can also buy excellent fresh stocks in supermarkets. Bouillon cubes and stock powders make a good storecupboard standby, but buy a good-quality brand as the flavor can vary enormously.

Time-savers

• Fresh stock can be stored in the freezer, so it's well worth keeping a batch at the ready. Make a large amount and freeze in several smaller containers so that you can defrost one quantity at a time.

• Another great time-saver is using canned pulses instead of dried. If using pulses in brine, rinse well and taste the soup before adding extra salt.
• When buying meat, fish, or shellfish, ask for it to be prepared for you ready for cooking, where possible.

Freezing soups

It can be useful to make a double batch of soup and freeze half for another day. As a general rule, smooth and chunky vegetable soups freeze well. Delicate broths containing tofu and noodles, and soups containing shellfish and eggs, will not freeze successfully. To freeze soups containing cream and cheese, it is best to freeze the soup before these ingredients are added; stir them into the soup after it has been defrosted and reheated. Fresh herbs and garnishes should always be added at the last minute, never frozen in the soup.

The finishing touch

When it comes to serving soup, presentation is everything. The same bowl of tomato soup can make a comforting meal when you're ill, a hearty and nutritious supper on a cold winter evening, or a stunning dish for entertaining, depending on how you present it. For convalescence, serve it plain and piping hot; for sustenance, scatter over strips of frazzled bacon and grated cheese and serve with chunks of crusty bread; and for sophistication, ladle the soup into elegant soup plates, add a swirl of cream, and scatter over fresh basil leaves.

Soups can be garnished in a hundred different ways. Simplest of all are fresh herbs; go for classic flavor combinations such as carrot and cilantro, or spinach and dill. Spices such as paprika can make a good garnish too. Dress up Asian-style soups with shreds of scallion and fiery chili, or top Mediterranean-style soups with shavings of Parmesan cheese. Crunchy fried shallots, colorful vegetable crisps, or tortilla chips make a great alternative to the classic crouton, and a spoonful of tangy salsa or fragrant pesto can make a sensational change to the traditional dollop of cream. When you're choosing a garnish, the golden rule is be creative and, above all, have fun!

Vegetable stock

makes **about 2 quarts**
preparation time **15 minutes**
cooking time **2½–3 hours**

2 quarts water
1 onion, unpeeled and halved
1 garlic clove, unpeeled and halved
1 carrot, roughly chopped
1 celery stick with leaves, roughly
    chopped
¼ small rutabaga, unpeeled and
    roughly chopped
1 leek, white and green parts,
    roughly chopped
1 parsley sprig
6 black peppercorns
1 bay leaf
1 bouquet garni
peelings of 1–2 scrubbed potatoes
outer leaves of cauliflower,
    cabbage, Brussels sprouts
    (optional)
salt

1 Combine the measured water with all the remaining ingredients in a deep pot. Bring to a boil, then lower the heat and simmer, covered, for 2½–3 hours. Skim off the scum with a slotted spoon from time to time.

2 Cool, then strain through a sieve, discarding all the vegetables and herbs in the sieve. Cover the stock closely and store in the refrigerator. Use within 3–4 days. This stock is suitable for freezing; if frozen, use within 4 months.

Chicken stock

makes **about 4 quarts**
preparation time **5–8 minutes**
cooking time **2½–3 hours**

1 whole chicken carcass
4 quarts water
1 teaspoon salt
1 Spanish onion, peeled and stuck
  with 4 cloves
2 celery sticks, chopped
2 carrots, roughly chopped
2 parsley sprigs
1 bouquet garni
1 bay leaf
8 black peppercorns

1 Put the carcass into a deep pot, cover with the measured water, and add the salt. Bring to a boil, skimming off the scum with a slotted spoon. Lower the heat, partially cover the pot, and simmer for 1 hour.

2 Add the onion, celery, carrots, parsley, bouquet garni, bay leaf, and peppercorns. Stir and continue simmering, partially covered, for 1½–2 hours. Add more water if the level drops below the bones.

3 Cool slightly. Remove the carcass, then strain the stock through a fine sieve into a bowl, discarding all the vegetables and herbs. After straining the stock, pick over the carcass, remove any meat still on the bones, and add it to the stock.

4 Leave to cool, then skim off the fat with a spoon or blot with paper towels. Cover the stock closely and store in the refrigerator. Use within 3 days. This stock is suitable for freezing; if frozen, use within 3 months.

Fish stock

makes **about 4 cups**
preparation time **5–8 minutes**
cooking time **30–40 minutes**

1 lb fish trimmings (bones, heads,
   tails, skins)
3³/₄ cups water
1 onion, quartered
2 celery sticks with leaves,
   roughly chopped
1 bay leaf
1 parsley sprig
¹/₄ teaspoon salt
6 black peppercorns
²/₃ cup dry white wine or cider

1 Put the fish trimmings into a large pot and cover with the measured water. Add all the remaining ingredients, stir well, and bring to a boil, skimming off the scum as it rises to the surface with a slotted spoon. Lower the heat and simmer, partially covered, for 30–40 minutes.

2 Remove the pot from the heat and strain the mixture through a sieve, discarding the fish trimmings and other ingredients. Cool, then cover closely and store in the refrigerator. Use within 2 days. This stock is suitable for freezing; if frozen, use within 2 months.

tip The heads, tails and bones of white fish, such as cod, haddock, plaice, hake, or whiting, make a good stock, but oily fish like mackerel and herring are not suitable.

Beef stock

makes **about 4 quarts**
preparation time **15 minutes**
cooking time **about 4 hours**

about 2 lb marrow and skin bones
4 quarts water
1 teaspoon salt
1 onion, quartered
2 celery sticks with leaves,
   roughly chopped
2 carrots, roughly chopped
4 parsley sprigs
1 bouquet garni
8 black peppercorns

1 Put the bones into a large pot. Cover them with the measured water and add the salt. Bring the liquid to a boil, skimming off any scum that rises to the surface with a slotted spoon. Lower the heat, partially cover the pan, and simmer over a low heat for 2 hours. Skim from time to time.

2 Add the remaining ingredients and continue to simmer for 2 hours. Add more water if the level drops below the bones.

3 Cool slightly, then strain the stock through a fine sieve into a bowl, discarding the bones, vegetables, herbs, and spices. Leave the stock to cool, then skim off the fat with a spoon or blot with paper towels. Cover the stock closely and store in the refrigerator. Use within 3 days. This stock is suitable for freezing; if frozen, use within 3 months.

Quick and Easy Soups

Simple, healthy, and requiring minimal time in the kitchen, these soups are the ultimate convenience food. The recipes in this chapter are ideal for light lunches, afterwork snacks, or impromptu meals for unexpected visitors.

Broccoli and cheese soup

serves **6**
preparation time **20 minutes**
cooking time **35–40 minutes**

2 lb broccoli
1/4 cup butter
1 onion, chopped
1 large potato, peeled and
  quartered
6 cups Vegetable Stock
  (see page 8)
1/2 cup light cream
1 tablespoon lemon juice
1 teaspoon Worcestershire sauce
a few drops of Tabasco sauce,
  or to taste
1 cup mature cheddar, grated
salt and pepper
watercress sprigs, to garnish

1 Remove all the tough stems and leaves from the broccoli. Cut off the stalks, peel them, and cut them into 1 inch pieces. Break the florets into very small pieces and set them aside.

2 Melt the butter in a large pot. Add the onion and broccoli stalks, and cook, covered, for 5 minutes over a moderate heat, stirring frequently.

3 Add the reserved broccoli florets, potato, and stock to the pan. Bring the mixture to a boil. Cook, partially covered, for 5 minutes. Season the mixture to taste with salt and pepper, and continue to cook over a moderate heat for 20 minutes, or until all the vegetables are soft.

4 Using a blender or food processor, puree the mixture until smooth, then transfer to a clean pot. Add the cream, lemon juice, Worcestershire sauce, and Tabasco to the pot. Simmer for 3–5 minutes. Do not let the soup boil or it will curdle. Just before serving, stir in the grated cheese and garnish each portion with watercress sprigs.

Parsnip and fennel soup

serves **4–6**
preparation time **10–15 minutes**
cooking time **35–40 minutes**

¼ cup butter
1 lb parsnips, cut into ¼ inch dice
1 lb fennel bulb, cut into small
   pieces of equal size
1 onion, chopped
3 tablespoons cornstarch
5 cups hot Vegetable or Chicken
   Stock (see pages 8 and 9)
⅔ cup heavy cream
salt and pepper

1 Melt the butter in a large pot. Add the parsnips, fennel, and onion, and cook over a moderate heat for 15 minutes, or until the vegetables are soft, stirring constantly.

2 In a small bowl, mix the cornstarch with ⅔ cup of the hot stock until thick and smooth. Fold the mixture into the vegetables, then pour in the remaining hot stock, stirring the soup constantly.

3 Bring the mixture to a boil, then lower the heat and simmer, partially covered, for 20 minutes, stirring frequently. Add salt and pepper to taste, stir in the cream, and heat through without boiling. Serve at once in warmed soup bowls.

Carrot and ginger soup

serves **4**
preparation time **20 minutes**
cooking time **25–30 minutes**

2 tablespoons olive oil
1 large onion, chopped
1–2 garlic cloves, crushed
1 tablespoon finely grated fresh
   root ginger
³/₄ lb carrots, sliced
3³/₄ cups Vegetable or Chicken
   Stock (see pages 8 and 9)
2 tablespoons lime or lemon juice
salt and pepper

To serve
sour cream
2 scallions, finely chopped

1 Heat the oil in a pot over a low heat. Add the onion, garlic, and ginger, and cook for 5–6 minutes, or until softened.

2 Add the carrots and stock, and bring to a boil, then reduce the heat and simmer for 15–20 minutes, or until the carrots are tender.

3 Puree the soup in a blender or food processor with the lime or lemon juice until smooth. Strain it through a sieve and return to the pot to reheat. Serve with a spoonful of sour cream in each bowl of soup and sprinkle with scallions.

Potato soup with parsley

serves **4**
preparation time **10 minutes**
cooking time **20 minutes**

6 cups Beef Stock (see page 11)
4 potatoes, coarsely grated
1 egg yolk
1 hard-boiled egg yolk, mashed
3 tablespoons light cream
½ cup grated Parmesan cheese
1 tablespoon finely chopped
   parsley
salt and pepper
1 cup croutons, to serve
   (see below)

1 Put the stock into a pot and bring to a boil. Sprinkle the potatoes with salt and pepper to taste, then drop them into the boiling stock. Cook for about 15 minutes, stirring from time to time.

2 Beat the egg yolk in a soup tureen and add the mashed hard-boiled egg yolk. Blend the cream, Parmesan, and parsley into the egg mixture, and whisk them together.

3 Carefully pour 1 cup of the stock into the egg mixture. Reheat the remaining stock and potatoes, and gradually add them to the soup tureen. Sprinkle with croutons and serve in warmed soup bowls.

tip To make croutons, cut the crusts off 2–3 slices of white bread, then cube the bread. Heat 1 tablespoon vegetable oil in a heavy-based frying pan and fry the bread cubes, turning and stirring frequently, for 1–2 minutes, or until golden and crisp.

Zucchini and mint soup

serves **4**
preparation time **20 minutes**
cooking time **20–25 minutes**

1/4 cup butter
1 small onion, chopped
1–2 garlic cloves, crushed
1 1/2 lb zucchini, diced
finely grated rind of 1 lemon
2 1/2 cups Vegetable or Chicken
   Stock (see pages 8 and 9),
   or water
2–3 tablespoons chopped mint
2 egg yolks
1/3 cup heavy cream
salt and pepper
light cream, to garnish

1 Melt the butter in a pot over a low heat. Add the onion and garlic, and cook for 5–6 minutes, or until softened. Stir in the zucchini and lemon rind, and cook for 5–10 minutes, or until tender. Add the stock or water and mint and bring to a boil, then lower the heat and simmer for 5 minutes.

2 Puree the soup in a blender or food processor until smooth, then strain through a sieve.

3 Immediately before serving, reheat the soup to just below boiling point. Mix together the egg yolks and heavy cream in a small bowl and whisk in a ladleful of the hot soup. Whisk this mixture back into the pan; do not let the soup boil or it will curdle. Season to taste with salt and pepper, and serve in warmed soup bowls. Drizzle with light cream before serving.

Pea, lettuce, and lemon soup with sesame croutons

serves **4**
preparation time **10 minutes**
cooking time **20 minutes**

2 tablespoons butter
1 large onion, finely chopped
3 cups frozen peas
2 Little Gem lettuces, roughly chopped
4 cups Vegetable or Chicken Stock (see pages 8 and 9)
grated rind and juice of ½ lemon
salt and pepper

Sesame croutons
2 thick slices of bread, cubed
1 tablespoon olive oil
1 tablespoon sesame seeds

1 To make the sesame croutons, brush the bread cubes with the oil and put in a roasting pan. Sprinkle with the sesame seeds and cook in a preheated oven at 400°F, for 10–15 minutes, or until golden.

2 Meanwhile, melt the butter in a large pot. Add the onion and cook for 5 minutes, or until beginning to soften. Add the peas, lettuce, stock, lemon rind and juice, and seasoning. Bring to a boil, then reduce the heat, cover and simmer for 10–15 minutes.

3 Let the soup cool slightly, then transfer to a blender or food processor and puree until smooth. Return the soup to the pot, adjust the seasoning if necessary, and heat through. Spoon into warmed soup bowls and sprinkle with the sesame croutons.

Spinach and broccoli soup

serves **4**
preparation time **10 minutes**
cooking time **20 minutes**

2 tablespoons olive oil
$1/4$ cup butter
1 onion, diced
1 garlic clove, finely chopped
2 potatoes, diced
$1/2$ lb broccoli, chopped
$5^1/2$ cups chopped spinach
$3^3/4$ cups Vegetable or Chicken
    Stock (see pages 8 and 9)
$1/4$ lb Gorgonzola cheese, crumbled
    into small pieces
juice of $1/2$ lemon
$1/2$ teaspoon grated nutmeg
salt and pepper
$3/4$ cup toasted pine nuts,
    to garnish
warm crusty bread, to serve

1 Heat the oil and butter in a pot, add the onion and garlic, and cook for 3 minutes. Add the potatoes, broccoli, spinach, and stock, and bring to a boil, then lower the heat, and simmer for 15 minutes.

2 Add the Gorgonzola to the soup with the lemon juice, nutmeg, and salt and pepper to taste. For a smooth consistency, puree the soup in a blender or food processor. Alternatively, it can be left with chunky pieces according to taste. Spoon into warmed soup bowls, garnish with toasted pine nuts, and serve with warm crusty bread.

Watercress soup with poached quails' eggs

serves **4**
preparation time **5 minutes**
cooking time **20–25 minutes**

¼ cup butter
1 onion, finely chopped
½ lb potatoes, cut into ½ inch
   cubes
2½ cups roughly chopped
   watercress
3¾ cups Vegetable or Chicken
   Stock (see pages 8 and 9)
1¼ cups light cream
12 quails' eggs
salt and pepper
½ cup Parmesan cheese, finely
   grated, to serve

1 Melt the butter in a large pot, add the onion and cook gently, without letting it color, for 8–10 minutes, or until well softened. Stir in the potatoes and watercress, cover and cook for 3–5 minutes, stirring once or twice, until the watercress has just wilted.

2 Add the stock, and season with salt and pepper. Bring to a boil, then lower the heat and simmer for 6–8 minutes, or until the potatoes are tender.

3 Puree the soup in a blender or food processor until smooth. Strain it through a sieve and return to the pan. Add the cream, adjust the seasoning to taste, and heat through without boiling.

4 Poach the quails' eggs in a saucepan of gently simmering water. Remove the eggs with a slotted spoon and drain well on paper towels. Place 3 eggs in each serving bowl. Ladle the watercress soup over the eggs and serve with the grated Parmesan.

Avgolemono

serves **4–6**

preparation time **about 10 minutes**

cooking time **25 minutes**

6 cups Vegetable or Chicken Stock
   (see pages 8 and 9)
$\frac{1}{3}$ cup long-grain white rice
2 eggs
2–3 tablespoons lemon juice
salt and pepper
1 tablespoon chopped parsley,
   to garnish (optional)

1 Combine the stock, $\frac{1}{2}$ teaspoon salt, and the rice in a pot. Bring the mixture to a boil. Stir, then lower the heat, cover and simmer for 20 minutes. Stir once more.

2 Beat the eggs in a small bowl, then whisk in the lemon juice. Add a ladleful of stock, beat, then add another ladleful of stock and beat again.

3 Bring the remaining stock and rice mixture to a boil. Briefly remove the pot from the heat, and add the egg and lemon mixture. Stir well, lower the heat, and simmer for 2 minutes, then add salt and pepper to taste. Sprinkle on the parsley, if desired. Serve immediately in warmed soup bowls.

Crab soup

serves **4–6**
preparation time **10 minutes**
cooking time **about 20 minutes**

4 cups Chicken Stock (see page 9)
1 inch piece of fresh ginger root,
    peeled and very finely chopped
2 ripe tomatoes, skinned, seeded,
    and very finely chopped
$\frac{1}{2}$ small red or green chili, seeded,
    and very finely chopped
2 tablespoons rice wine or
    dry sherry
1 tablespoon rice wine vinegar or
    white wine or cider vinegar
$\frac{1}{2}$ teaspoon sugar
1 tablespoon cornstarch
about $\frac{2}{3}$ cup white crab meat,
    defrosted and drained
    thoroughly if frozen
salt and pepper
2 scallions, finely sliced
    lengthwise, to garnish

1 Put the stock into a large pot with the ginger, tomatoes, chili, rice wine or sherry, vinegar, and sugar. Bring to a boil, then cover, lower the heat, and simmer for about 10 minutes to let the flavors mingle and mellow.

2 Blend the cornstarch to a paste with a little cold water, then pour it into the soup and stir to mix. Simmer, stirring, for 1–2 minutes, or until the soup thickens.

3 Add the crab meat, stir gently to mix, then heat through for 2–3 minutes. Taste and add salt and pepper if necessary. Serve piping hot in warmed soup bowls, sprinkled with the sliced scallions.

tip Frozen white crab meat is convenient to use and it can be found in large supermarkets. Alternatively, you can buy a whole cooked fresh crab from a fishmonger and have the meat removed for you.

Chicken and coconut milk soup

serves **4**
preparation time **6 minutes**
cooking time **10 minutes**

1¼ cups Chicken Stock
   (see page 9)
3 Kaffir lime leaves, torn
½ lemon grass stalk, obliquely
   sliced
1 inch piece of galangal, peeled
   and finely sliced
⅓ cup coconut milk
4 tablespoons Thai fish sauce
1 teaspoon palm sugar or light
   muscovado sugar
3 tablespoons lime juice
¼ lb chicken, skinned and cut into
   bite-size pieces
2 tablespoons chili oil or 2 small
   chilies, finely sliced (optional)

1 Heat the stock in a pot, then stir in the lime leaves, lemon grass, and galangal. As the stock is simmering, add the coconut milk, fish sauce, sugar, and lime juice, and stir well.

2 Add the chicken and simmer for 5 minutes.

3 Just before serving, add the chili oil or chilies, if desired. Stir again and serve in warmed soup bowls.

Pork ball and tofu soup

serves **4**
preparation time **10 minutes**
cooking time **12–13 minutes**

2¹/₂ cups Chicken Stock
   (see page 9)
1 garlic clove, finely chopped
4 garlic cloves, halved
¹/₂ teaspoon ground black pepper
8 fresh cilantro roots
1 cup silken tofu, cut into
   1 inch slices
1 sheet roasted laver seaweed,
   torn into shreds
2 tablespoons light soy sauce
fresh cilantro leaves, to garnish

Pork balls
¹/₂ cup ground pork
1 tablespoon light soy sauce
¹/₂ teaspoon ground black pepper

1 Heat the stock with the chopped and halved garlic, pepper, and cilantro in a pot. While the soup is heating, make the pork balls.

2 Mix together the pork, soy sauce, and pepper, then form the mixture into small balls. Drop them into the soup and simmer gently for 6–7 minutes.

3 Add the tofu, laver, and soy sauce, stir for 30 seconds, then serve the soup in warmed bowls, garnished with cilantro leaves.

Shrimp and lemon grass soup

serves **4**
preparation time **25 minutes**
cooking time **20 minutes**

$^3/_4$ lb raw shrimp
3 lemon grass stalks, cut into
   1 inch pieces
5 cups water
1 tomato, quartered and seeded
2 x 7 oz cans straw mushrooms,
   drained
6 Kaffir lime leaves
1 scallion, chopped
1$^1/_2$ cups bean sprouts
juice of 3 limes
2 small red chilies, finely sliced
4 tablespoons Vietnamese or Thai
   fish sauce
salt and pepper
fresh cilantro leaves, to garnish

1 Peel and devein the shrimp and set aside the shells. Cut off the white part of the lemon grass stalks, reserving the tops. Flatten the lemon grass stalks with a cleaver or pestle.

2 Heat the measured water in a pot and add the shrimp shells and the lemon grass tops. Bring the water slowly to a boil, strain and return to the pot. Add the flattened lemon grass, tomato, straw mushrooms, and lime leaves. Bring back to a boil, then lower the heat to a simmer and cook for 3–4 minutes.

3 Add the shrimp and, when they have changed color, add the scallion, bean sprouts, lime juice, chilies, and fish sauce. Season to taste with salt and pepper and stir well.

4 Serve in individual warmed soup bowls, sprinkled with cilantro leaves.

Classic Soups

Everyone has a favorite soup and these recipes show you how to make them with minimum fuss. From the creamy *Vichyssoise* and the chunky *Minestrone*, to the spicy *Mulligatawny* and the luxurious *Shrimp Bisque*.

Tomato soup with croutons

serves **4**
preparation time **10 minutes**
cooking time **40 minutes**

4 tablespoons olive oil
1 onion, chopped
3 garlic cloves, crushed
1½ lb tomatoes, peeled and
    chopped
4 cups Vegetable or Chicken Stock
    (see pages 8 and 9)
salt and pepper
croutons, to serve (see page 18)
a few basil leaves, chopped,
    to garnish

1 Heat half the oil in a large pot. Add the onion
and garlic, and cook gently for 4–6 minutes, or until
golden but not brown. Add the tomatoes and cook for
5 minutes, then gradually stir in the stock. Add salt
and pepper to taste, then simmer for 30 minutes.

2 Meanwhile, make the croutons.

3 Add the croutons and the basil to the soup and
serve immediately in warmed soup bowls.

Pumpkin soup

serves **6**

preparation time **about**
10 minutes

cooking time **40–45 minutes**

¼ cup butter
1½ lb pumpkin, peeled, seeded,
    and cut into large pieces
⅔ cup warm water
¼ teaspoon grated nutmeg
pinch of dried thyme
6 cups milk
⅓ cup long-grain white rice
salt and pepper
croutons, to garnish (see page 18)

1 Melt the butter in a large pot. Add the pumpkin, stir well, and cook over a low to moderate heat for 10 minutes. Add the measured warm water, nutmeg, thyme, and salt and pepper to taste. Cover and cook over a high heat until the pumpkin is soft.

2 Puree the pumpkin mixture in a blender or food processor, with a little of the milk if necessary, until smooth. Transfer to a clean pot.

3 Add the remaining milk and rice to the pumpkin puree in the pot. Stir well and cook, covered, for 30 minutes, or until the rice is tender, stirring from time to time. Serve the pumpkin soup in warmed bowls, garnished with croutons.

Roasted pepper soup
with black pepper cream

serves **4**

preparation time **20 minutes**

cooking time **about 1 hour**

6 large red or yellow bell peppers

4 leeks, white and pale green parts
  only, thinly sliced

3 tablespoons olive oil

3 cups Vegetable or Chicken Stock
  (see pages 8 and 9)

2 teaspoons black peppercorns

1/4 cup mascarpone cheese

1/4 cup milk

salt and pepper

toasted crusty bread, to serve

1 Put the peppers into a large roasting pan and roast in a preheated oven, 475°F, for 20–30 minutes, turning once, until they begin to char. Remove the peppers from the oven, put them into a plastic bag and close it tightly. Leave for 10 minutes to steam.

2 Put the leeks into a bowl of cold water to soak for 5 minutes.

3 Remove the peppers from the bag and peel off the skins, then pull out the stalks—the seeds should come with them. Halve the peppers, scrape out any remaining seeds, and roughly chop the flesh. Swish the leeks around in the water to loosen any soil, then drain and rinse well.

4 Heat the oil in a large pot. Add the leeks and cook gently for 10 minutes until soft but not colored. Add the peppers, stock, and a little salt and pepper. Bring the mixture to a boil, then lower the heat and simmer for 20 minutes.

5 Pound or grind the black peppercorns as finely as possible. Beat the mascarpone with the milk and pepper. Season with salt, cover and chill in the refrigerator until needed.

6 Puree the soup in a blender or food processor, then pass it through a sieve into the rinsed-out pot. Reheat, taste and adjust the seasoning if necessary. Serve the soup in warmed bowls with dollops of the pepper cream and slices of toasted crusty bread.

Vichyssoise

serves **6**

preparation time **15 minutes**, plus chilling

cooking time **about 35–40 minutes**

1/4 cup butter

2 lb leeks, white parts only, finely sliced

1 onion, chopped

4 cups Vegetable or Chicken Stock (see pages 8 and 9)

pinch of grated nutmeg

1 1/2 lb old potatoes, cubed

2 1/2 cups milk

1 1/4 cups light cream

2/3 cup heavy cream, chilled

salt and white pepper

2 tablespoons snipped fresh chives, to garnish

1 Melt the butter in a pot. Add the leeks and onion, and cook over a moderate heat for 5 minutes, stirring constantly. Do not let the vegetables change color.

2 Add the stock, nutmeg, potatoes, and salt and pepper to taste. Bring the mixture to a boil, then lower the heat and cook, partially covered, for 25 minutes. Pour in the milk and simmer for 5–8 minutes. Cool slightly.

3 Puree the mixture in a blender or food processor until smooth, then rub it through a sieve into a bowl. Add the light cream, stir well, and cover the bowl closely. Chill in the refrigerator for at least 3 hours.

4 Just before serving, swirl in the heavy cream and add more salt and pepper if required. Serve in chilled bowls, garnishing each portion with a generous sprinkling of snipped chives.

Leek and potato soup

serves **4–6**
preparation time **15 minutes**
cooking time **40 minutes**

2 tablespoons butter
2 large leeks, finely sliced
1/2 lb potatoes, roughly diced
1 onion, roughly chopped
3 cups Vegetable or Chicken Stock
  (see pages 8 and 9), or water
1 1/4 cups milk
salt and pepper
1 tablespoon snipped chives,
  to garnish

1 Melt the butter in a large pot. Add the leeks, potatoes, and onion, and stir well to coat with the butter. Cover tightly with a piece of wax paper and cook over a very gentle heat for about 15 minutes, or until the vegetables have softened, stirring frequently to prevent them from browning.

2 Add the stock or water and milk, and season to taste with salt and pepper. Bring to a boil, then lower the heat and simmer gently for about 20 minutes, or until the vegetables are tender.

3 Puree the mixture in a blender or food processor until smooth, then transfer it to a clean pot.

4 Adjust the seasoning if necessary and heat until very hot, then pour the soup into warmed bowls. Garnish with chives and serve.

Mushroom soup with crispy bacon

serves **4–6**
preparation time **15 minutes**
cooking time **25–30 minutes**

$^{1}/_{4}$ cup butter
1 onion, finely chopped
1 garlic clove, finely chopped
$^{3}/_{4}$ lb mushrooms, thinly sliced
2 tablespoons all-purpose flour
2$^{1}/_{2}$ cups Chicken Stock
   (see page 9)
$^{2}/_{3}$ cup milk
1 tablespoon Manzanilla sherry
   (optional)
$^{2}/_{3}$ cup light cream
4 rindless bacon slices, cooked
   until crisp and broken into
   small pieces
salt and pepper
chervil sprigs, to garnish

1 Melt the butter in a large pot. Add the onion, garlic, and mushrooms, and cook until soft and beginning to color. Sprinkle on the flour and stir to combine. Gradually pour on the stock and milk, stirring well to blend. Bring to a boil, then lower the heat and simmer for about 15–20 minutes.

2 Add salt and pepper to taste, along with the sherry, if using, and half the cream. Reheat the soup without boiling, then pour into warmed soup bowls. Whip the remaining cream until it is just holding its shape, then spoon a little on top of each bowl of soup. Sprinkle with the bacon pieces and garnish with chervil sprigs.

tip A mixture of cultivated and wild mushrooms gives the soup a very special flavor. For a smoother soup, puree it before adding the cream.

French onion soup

serves **6**
preparation time **10 minutes**
cooking time **about 35 minutes**

¼ cup butter
1 lb Spanish onions, sliced into
  fairly thick rings
¾ cup all-purpose flour
5 cups Vegetable or Beef Stock
  (see pages 8 and 11)
1 tablespoon Cognac (optional)
½ teaspoon Dijon mustard
salt and pepper

To garnish
6 slices of French bread
¾ cup Gruyère cheese, grated
finely chopped parsley

1 Melt the butter in a large pot. Add the onions and cook over a moderate heat, stirring constantly, until soft and pale gold in color. Sprinkle in the flour and stir for about 1 minute, then gradually pour in the stock. Bring the mixture to a boil, stirring constantly, and add salt and pepper to taste.

2 Lower the heat and simmer for 20–25 minutes. Stir in the Cognac, if using, and the mustard. Keep the soup hot.

3 Broil the bread for the garnish until it is lightly browned, then sprinkle each slice with the grated Gruyère. Pour the soup into heatproof bowls and float a slice of cheese-topped bread in each bowl. Put the bowls under a preheated broiler until the cheese melts and bubbles. Sprinkle with chopped parsley and serve the soup immediately.

Ham and pea soup

serves **6**
preparation time **10 minutes**,
plus soaking
cooking time **1¼ hours**

½ lb yellow or green split peas,
   soaked for 4–6 hours in cold
   water to cover
¼ cup butter
1 large onion, roughly chopped
1 large carrot, roughly chopped
4 thick bacon slices, approximately
   6 oz, derinded and diced
1 small bay leaf
1 ham bone
5 cups water
2 tablespoons snipped chives
salt and pepper

1 Drain the split peas in a colander and discard the soaking water.

2 Melt the butter in a pot. Add the onion, carrot, and two-thirds of the bacon, and cook gently for about 15 minutes, or until soft. Add the drained split peas, bay leaf, ham bone, and measured water. Bring to a boil, then lower the heat, and simmer gently for 1 hour.

3 Remove from the heat and discard the ham bone. Season with salt and pepper, if necessary. Return the pot to the heat. Cook the remaining bacon in a hot frying pan until crisp, then add to the soup along with half the chives. Serve the soup in warmed bowls garnished with the remaining chives.

Green lentil and bacon soup

serves **6–8**
preparation time **15–20 minutes**
cooking time **1¼ hours**

2 tablespoons butter
¼ lb rindless smoked lean bacon,
   finely chopped
1 garlic clove, finely chopped
1 onion, finely chopped
2¼ cups green lentils, rinsed
   and drained
1 celery stick, sliced
1 large carrot, diced
1 parsley sprig
1 thyme sprig or ¼ teaspoon
   dried thyme
1 bay leaf
5 cups Chicken Stock (see page 9)
3¾ cups water
1 lemon slice
salt and pepper

1 Melt the butter in a large pot. Add the bacon, garlic, and onion, and cook over a moderate to high heat for 5 minutes, stirring constantly.

2 Lower the heat and add the lentils, celery, carrot, parsley, thyme, and bay leaf to the pot. Pour in the stock and the measured water. Bring the mixture to a boil, skimming off the scum as it rises to the surface with a slotted spoon. Add the lemon slice.

3 Lower the heat, cover and simmer for 55–60 minutes, stirring occasionally. If the soup is too thick, stir in a little more water. Carefully remove and discard the parsley and thyme sprigs, bay leaf, and lemon slice. Add salt and pepper to taste if necessary.

4 Measure 2½ cups of the soup and puree it in a blender or food processor until smooth. Return the puree to the soup, stir well, and cook over a moderate heat for 5 minutes. Serve in warmed soup bowls.

Turkey and vegetable soup

serves **8**
preparation time **25 minutes**
cooking time **about 2 hours**

1 large turkey drumstick, about
   1½ lb
2¾ quarts water
1 small unpeeled onion, studded
   with 4 cloves plus 1 large onion,
   peeled and chopped
2 sprigs of parsley
1 bouquet garni
1 teaspoon salt
1 sprig of thyme, or ¼ teaspoon
   dried thyme
1 sprig of marjoram, or ½ teaspoon
   dried marjoram
3 carrots, chopped
2 celery sticks, sliced
1¼ cups red lentils, rinsed and
   drained
½ lb potatoes, peeled and cut into
   ½ inch cubes
3 leeks, sliced
3 turnips, peeled and cut into
   ½ inch cubes
2 tablespoons light soy sauce
pepper
3–4 tablespoons finely chopped
   fresh parsley, to garnish

1 Place the drumstick in a large pot. Add the measured water, the studded onion, parsley sprigs, bouquet garni, salt, thyme, and marjoram. Bring the mixture to a boil, lower the heat, and simmer, partially covered, for 45 minutes.

2 Add the chopped onion, carrots, and celery. Cook for 30 minutes over a low to moderate heat, then add the lentils, potatoes, leeks, and turnips. Cook, until all the vegetables are tender. Remove the drumstick and let it cool. Remove and discard the bouquet garni, the studded onion with cloves, and any parsley, thyme, or marjoram stems.

3 Cut the turkey meat off the bone, discarding the skin. Carefully remove any small bones. Cut the meat into small pieces and return it to the pot. Add the soy sauce to the pot with pepper to taste. Heat the soup thoroughly, and serve in a soup tureen, garnished with the parsley.

Cream of chicken soup

serves **6**
preparation time **15 minutes**
cooking time **1¼ hours**

1 chicken carcass
1 onion
1 bouquet garni
4 cups Chicken Stock (see page 9)
¼ lb cooked chicken
1¼ cups milk
½ cup all-purpose flour
2 tablespoons water
1 tablespoon lemon juice
¼ teaspoon grated nutmeg
salt and pepper

To garnish
croutons (see page 18)
Italian parsley sprigs
grated nutmeg

To serve
⅔ cup light cream
lemon wedges

1 Put the carcass, onion, and bouquet garni into a pot with the stock. Simmer for about 1 hour. Strain the liquid and return it to the pot.

2 Neatly dice the cooked chicken meat and add to the stock with the milk. Blend the flour with the measured water, then slowly add the mixture to the stock, stirring constantly. Bring to a boil, then lower the heat and simmer gently for 10 minutes. Season the soup with lemon juice, nutmeg, and salt and pepper to taste.

3 Pour the soup into warmed soup bowls. Pour over the cream and garnish with croutons, Italian parsley sprigs, and some grated nutmeg. Serve with lemon wedges on the side.

Minestrone

serves **8–10**

preparation time **about 30 minutes**, plus soaking

cooking time **about 2¾ hours**

1¼ cups dried haricot beans, soaked overnight in cold water to cover

3 tablespoons olive oil

2 onions, finely chopped

2 garlic cloves, finely chopped

2 rindless streaky bacon slices, finely chopped

6 tomatoes, peeled and chopped

2 quarts water

2½ cups Beef Stock (see page 11)

1 zucchini, diced

1 tablespoon chopped fresh marjoram or 1 teaspoon dried marjoram

1 teaspoon chopped fresh thyme or ½ teaspoon dried thyme

2 tablespoons tomato paste

2 carrots, diced

2 celery sticks, finely sliced

½ Savoy cabbage, finely shredded

½ lb fresh shelled or frozen peas

½ cup dried spaghetti, broken into small pieces or small pasta shapes

1 tablespoon chopped parsley

1¼ cups grated Parmesan cheese

salt and pepper

1 Drain the beans thoroughly in a colander, then rinse under cold running water, and drain again.

2 Heat the oil in a large pot. Add the onions, garlic, and bacon, and cook over a moderate heat until the onions are transparent, but not brown, and the bacon is crisp.

3 Stir in the tomatoes, the measured water, and stock, then add the zucchini, beans, marjoram, thyme, and tomato paste. Bring the mixture to a boil, skimming off the scum as it rises to the surface with a slotted spoon. Lower the heat and simmer, covered, for about 2 hours, or until the beans are tender.

4 Add the carrots and celery, and cook over a moderate heat for 15 minutes, then add the cabbage, peas, and pasta. Cook for 15–18 minutes, or until the vegetables and pasta are tender.

5 Add a little more water if the soup is too thick. Add the parsley, season to taste with salt and pepper, and stir in ½ cup of the Parmesan. Serve the soup immediately in warmed bowls, with the remaining Parmesan served separately.

Mulligatawny

serves **6–8**
preparation time **15–20 minutes**
cooking time **30–35 minutes**

1 onion, chopped
2 garlic cloves, chopped
1 inch piece of fresh ginger root,
    peeled and chopped
¼ teaspoon cayenne pepper
1 teaspoon ground coriander
½ teaspoon ground cumin
1 teaspoon ground turmeric
4 teaspoons vegetable oil
3 boneless, skinless chicken
    breasts, halved
5 cups Chicken Stock (see page 9)
5 cups water
⅓ cup long-grain white rice
⅔ cup red lentils
1 tablespoon lemon juice
2 tablespoons grated creamed
    coconut
salt
6–8 lemon slices, to garnish

1 In a blender or food processor, puree the onion, garlic, and ginger with the cayenne, coriander, cumin, and turmeric to a smooth paste, scraping down the sides of the pitcher or bowl with a wooden or plastic spatula from time to time.

2 Heat the oil in a large pot and cook the onion paste over a moderate heat, stirring, for 2–3 minutes. Add the chicken breasts and cook, stirring, for 1–2 minutes.

3 Slowly pour in the stock and measured water, stirring constantly. Add the rice and lentils, and simmer for 15–20 minutes, or until the rice is tender.

4 Remove the chicken, cut it into small pieces and set aside. Puree 3¾ cups of the soup mixture in a blender or food processor, then return it to the remaining soup in the pan. Add a little water if the soup is too thick, and salt to taste.

5 Stir well, then add the lemon juice, coconut, and reserved chicken pieces. Stir again and heat thoroughly without boiling for 3–5 minutes. Serve in warmed soup bowls, garnishing each portion with a lemon slice.

Bouillabaisse

serves **6–8**

preparation time **about 35 minutes**

cooking time **35–40 minutes**

4 tablespoons olive oil

2 garlic cloves, finely chopped

2 onions, chopped

1 lb prepared mackerel, cut into chunks

1 lb whiting fillet, cut into chunks

1 lb haddock or cod fillet, cut into chunks

½ lb raw shrimp, peeled

6 tomatoes, peeled and chopped

½ teaspoon saffron threads

6 cups hot Fish Stock (see page 10)

1 bay leaf

3 parsley sprigs

10–12 live mussels, scrubbed and debearded

6–8 slices of French bread

salt and pepper

2 tablespoons finely chopped parsley, to garnish

1 Heat the oil in a large pot. Add the garlic and onions, and cook, covered, for 3–5 minutes, or until the onions are transparent but not brown. Add the mackerel, whiting, and haddock or cod, and cook, uncovered, over a moderate heat for 10 minutes. Stir from time to time.

2 Add the shrimp and tomatoes. Dissolve the saffron threads in the hot stock, and add to the pot with the bay leaf, parsley sprigs, and salt and pepper to taste. Stir and bring the mixture to a boil. Lower the heat and simmer, covered, for 15 minutes, then add the mussels and continue cooking for 10 minutes, or until the fish is cooked.

3 Remove and discard the bay leaf and parsley sprigs and any mussels that have not opened. Put the bread into a warmed soup tureen and ladle in the soup. Sprinkle with the chopped parsley before serving.

Clam chowder

serves **6–8**
preparation time **25–45 minutes**
cooking time **35–40 minutes**

48–60 live clams in closed shells
  (discard any that do not shut
  immediately when sharply
  tapped)
2½ tablespoons butter
¼ lb smoked streaky bacon,
  derinded and diced
2 large onions, finely chopped
2 celery sticks, diced
1–2 leeks, sliced
2 tablespoons finely chopped
  parsley, plus extra to garnish
2 bay leaves
leaves from 1 thyme sprig
3¾ cups water
ground nutmeg
4–5 medium potatoes, diced
2 tablespoons all-purpose flour
1–2 teaspoons Worcestershire
  sauce
finely ground sea salt (optional)
  and pepper

1 Put the clams on a baking sheet in a preheated oven, 400°F, for 2–3 minutes, or until they open slightly, then remove them and prise the shells apart. Open the shells over a bowl to catch all the clam juice. Snip off the inedible black-tipped necks (which resemble a tube), roughly chop the coral-colored and pink flesh, and leave the softer body meat whole.

2 Melt half the butter in a large pot. Add the bacon and cook for about 5 minutes, or until the fat starts to run. Add the onions, cover, and cook gently for 10 minutes. Add the celery, leeks, parsley, bay leaves, and thyme, and cook for 5 minutes. Add the reserved clam juice, the measured water, nutmeg and pepper to taste, and the potatoes. Stir well, taste and season with salt if necessary. Simmer gently for about 10 minutes, or until the potatoes are almost tender.

3 Meanwhile, cream the flour with the remaining butter to a smooth paste and reserve. Add the clams to the pan and simmer very gently for 3–4 minutes. Do not boil the soup or the clams will be tough and rubbery. Add a piece of the butter and flour paste to the pan, stirring well. When it has been fully incorporated, stir in a little more, and continue until all the paste has been added. Stir for another 3–4 minutes, or until the soup thickens slightly.

4 Increase the heat briefly for 10 seconds, then remove from the heat. Add the Worcestershire sauce, stir, and serve immediately in warmed soup bowls, garnished with parsley.

Shrimp bisque

serves **4**
preparation time **20 minutes**
cooking time **35–45 minutes**

¼ cup butter
1 small carrot, finely chopped
½ small onion, finely chopped
½ celery stick, finely chopped
1 lb raw shrimp in their shells
1 cup dry white wine
2 tablespoons brandy
5 cups Fish Stock (see page 10)
1 bouquet garni
1 oz long-grain white rice
⅓ cup heavy cream
pinch of cayenne pepper
salt and pepper
4 tablespoons chopped parsley,
   to garnish

1 Melt the butter in a large heavy-based pot. Add the carrot, onion, and celery, and cook, stirring occasionally, for 8–10 minutes, or until softened and lightly golden. Increase the heat, add the shrimp, and cook for 3–4 minutes, or until the shells turn pink all over.

2 Add the wine and brandy, and bring to a boil, then lower the heat and simmer for 3–4 minutes, or until the shrimp are cooked. Remove the shrimp and leave to cool slightly. When cool enough to handle, peel the shrimp, reserving the shells. Remove the black veins running down the back, chop the flesh, and set aside.

3 Bring the liquid back to a boil and boil rapidly for 2–3 minutes, or until reduced by one-third. Add the reserved shrimp shells with the stock, bouquet garni, and rice. Bring to a boil, then lower the heat and simmer gently for 15–20 minutes, or until the rice is tender.

4 Remove and discard the bouquet garni. Puree the soup, including the shells, in a blender or food processor with three-quarters of the shrimp meat. Strain through a fine sieve into a clean pan, pressing with the back of a ladle to push through as much liquid as you can. Add the cream and cayenne, and season to taste with salt and pepper.

5 Bring the soup back to a boil, then lower the heat. Add the reserved chopped shrimp, and cook for 1–2 minutes, or until heated through. Serve in warmed soup bowls, sprinkled with the chopped parsley.

Summer Soups

Whether warm or chilled, soup can be surprisingly refreshing on a hot summer's day. Packed with Mediterranean flavors, light ingredients, and fragrant herbs, these elegant dishes are guaranteed to impress.

Chicory soup

serves **4**
preparation time **5 minutes**
cooking time **about 40 minutes**

¹/₃ cup butter
1 onion, diced
2 chicory heads, finely chopped
3 tablespoons dry white wine
4 cups milk
1 cup Vegetable or Chicken Stock
  (see pages 8 and 9)
2 tablespoons cornstarch
2 tablespoons grated Parmesan
  cheese
8 slices of stale bread, buttered
salt and pepper

1 Melt ¼ cup of the butter in a pot over a low heat.
Add the onion and cook until golden. Add the chicory
and cook slowly in the butter for 10 minutes, then
season to taste with salt and pepper. Pour in the
wine, and when this has evaporated, stir in most of
the milk and the stock. Bring slowly to a boil. Mix the
cornstarch with the remaining milk and add to the pan,
stirring constantly to avoid lumps.

2 Cook for 25 minutes over a moderate heat, then
whisk in the grated Parmesan and the remaining
butter, cut into pieces.

3 Meanwhile, toast the stale bread in a preheated
oven, 400°F, for about 10 minutes, or until golden
brown. Put the toast into warmed soup bowls and
pour the soup over. Serve hot.

Celery, carrot, and apple soup

serves **6**
preparation time **15 minutes**
cooking time **about 1 hour**

¼ cup unsalted butter
1 lb celery, sliced
1 lb carrots, chopped
½ lb eating apples, peeled, cored,
　and roughly chopped
5 cups Vegetable Stock
　(see page 8)
1 teaspoon paprika
cayenne pepper, to taste
1 tablespoon chopped fresh basil
　leaves or 1 teaspoon dried basil
1 bay leaf
1 teaspoon freshly grated ginger
　root
salt and ground white pepper

To garnish
chopped celery leaves
paprika

1 Melt the butter in a large pot, and add the celery, carrots, and apple. Cover with a tight-fitting lid and cook over a low heat for 15 minutes, stirring occasionally.

2 Add the stock, paprika, cayenne, basil, bay leaf, and ginger. Bring to a boil, then lower the heat and simmer, partially covered, for 40–45 minutes, or until the vegetables and apple are very soft.

3 Puree the mixture in a blender or food processor until smooth. Strain it through a sieve back into the pot and season to taste with salt and pepper. Reheat the soup. Serve the soup in warmed bowls, garnishing each portion with a few chopped celery leaves and a light sprinkling of paprika.

Jerusalem artichoke soup with artichoke crisps

serves **4**
preparation time **25 minutes**
cooking time **30 minutes**

1 small lemon
1¼ lb Jerusalem artichokes
¼ cup butter
1 onion, chopped
1 garlic clove, crushed
1 celery stick, chopped
leaves from 1 lemon thyme sprig
4 cups Vegetable or Chicken Stock
  (see pages 8 and 9)
vegetable oil, for deep-frying
¾ cup light cream or milk
3 tablespoons finely grated
  Parmesan cheese
salt and pepper
Italian parsley leaves, to garnish

1 Finely grate the rind from the lemon and set it aside. Squeeze the juice and put it into a large bowl of cold water. Carefully peel the artichokes; reserve 2 and chop the rest into ¾ inch pieces, dropping them into the lemon water as you prepare them to prevent discoloration.

2 Melt the butter in a large pot. Add the onion, garlic, celery, thyme, and reserved lemon rind. Cook gently, without letting them color, for 6–8 minutes, or until softened. Drain the chopped artichokes and add to the pot with the stock. Season to taste with salt and pepper and bring to a boil. Lower the heat and simmer for about 15 minutes, or until the artichokes are tender.

3 To prepare the artichoke crisps, drain the 2 reserved whole artichokes, slice them thinly, and dry well on paper towels. Heat some oil in a deep pot to 350–375°F, or until a cube of bread browns in 30 seconds. Add the artichoke slices in batches and fry until crisp and golden. Drain well on paper towels.

4 Puree the soup in a blender or food processor until smooth. Strain the soup through a sieve and return to the pan. Add the cream or milk, and a little water if too thick. Season to taste and bring back to a boil. Stir in the finely grated Parmesan and serve in warmed bowls, sprinkled with the artichoke crisps and garnished with Italian parsley leaves.

Heart of artichoke soup with dill

serves **4–6**
preparation time **15–20 minutes**
cooking time **about 35 minutes**

¼ cup butter
1 onion, chopped
1 garlic clove, chopped
1 celery stick, sliced
14 oz can artichoke hearts, drained
5 cups Vegetable or Chicken Stock
   (see pages 8 and 9)
1 tablespoon lemon juice
3 tablespoons chopped dill
2 tablespoons all-purpose flour
⅔ cup light cream
salt and ground white pepper
4–6 dill sprigs, to garnish

1 Melt the butter in a pot. Add the onion, garlic, and celery, and cook, covered, over a moderate heat for 10–12 minutes, or until all the vegetables are soft. Stir from time to time.

2 Add the artichoke hearts, replace the lid, and cook for about 3 minutes. Pour in 4 cups of the stock and the lemon juice. Stir in 1 tablespoon of the dill, then cook, covered, over a moderate heat for 15 minutes.

3 Puree the mixture in a blender or food processor until smooth. Transfer to a clean pot.

4 Mix the flour with the remaining stock in a small bowl, adding a little water if necessary. Reheat the soup, whisk in the flour mixture, and stir until the soup thickens slightly. Add the remaining dill. Season to taste with salt and pepper, then add the cream. Heat thoroughly but do not let the soup boil, or it will curdle. Serve in warmed soup bowls, garnished with dill sprigs.

Cream of corn soup

serves **4–6**
preparation time **5–10 minutes**
cooking time **about 30 minutes**

3 tablespoons butter
1 onion, chopped
2 potatoes, diced
1/4 cup all-purpose flour
3 3/4 cups milk
1 bay leaf
2 x 11 1/2 oz cans corn, drained
2 tablespoons heavy cream
salt and freshly ground
   white pepper
crumbled fried bacon, to garnish
garlic croutons, to serve
   (see page 107)

1 Melt the butter in a large pot. Add the onion and cook over a low heat, stirring frequently, for 5 minutes without browning. Add the potatoes and cook for 2 minutes.

2 Stir in the flour, then gradually add the milk, stirring constantly. Bring to a boil. Add the bay leaf and season to taste with salt and pepper. Add half the corn, cover and simmer for 15–20 minutes.

3 Remove and discard the bay leaf, and set the soup aside to cool slightly. Puree it in a blender or food processor until smooth. Return to the pan, add the remaining corn, and heat through.

4 Stir in the cream and sprinkle over the bacon. Serve the soup in warmed bowls with the garlic croutons.

Fennel and lemon soup with black olive gremolata

serves **4**
preparation time **20 minutes**
cooking time **about 40 minutes**

¼ cup olive oil
3 fat salad onions, chopped
½ lb fennel, trimmed, cored, and
    thinly sliced (reserve any green
    fronds for the gremolata)
1 potato, diced
finely grated rind and juice of
    1 lemon
3 cups Vegetable or Chicken Stock
    (see pages 8 and 9)
salt and pepper

Black olive gremolata
1 small garlic clove, finely chopped
finely grated rind of 1 lemon
4 tablespoons chopped parsley
finely chopped green fronds from
    the fennel
16 Greek-style black olives, pitted
    and chopped

1 Heat the oil in a large pot. Add the onions and cook for 5–10 minutes, or until beginning to soften. Add the fennel, potato, and lemon rind, and cook for 5 minutes. Pour in the stock and bring to a boil. Lower the heat, cover and simmer for about 25 minutes, or until the vegetables are tender.

2 Meanwhile, to make the gremolata, mix together the garlic, lemon rind, parsley, and fennel fronds, then stir in the olives. Cover and chill in the refrigerator.

3 Puree the soup in a blender or food processor and pass it through a sieve to remove any strings of fennel. The soup should not be too thick, so add more stock if necessary. Return it to the rinsed-out pot. Taste and season well with salt, pepper, and plenty of lemon juice. Pour into warmed soup bowls and sprinkle each serving with a portion of the gremolata, to be stirred in before eating.

Mint, cucumber, and green pea soup

serves **6**
preparation time **15 minutes**,
plus chilling (if serving cold)
cooking time **25–30 minutes**

¼ cup butter
1 lb cucumbers, peeled, seeded,
   and cut into ½ inch pieces
½ lb shelled fresh or frozen peas
pinch of sugar
¼ teaspoon white pepper
3 tablespoons finely chopped mint
5 cups Vegetable or Chicken Stock
   (see pages 8 and 9)
1¼ cups roughly chopped potatoes
⅔ cup heavy cream (chilled, if the
   soup is to be served cold)
salt

1 Melt the butter in a large pot. Add the cucumbers and cook over a moderate heat for 5 minutes, stirring occasionally. Add the peas, sugar, pepper, and 2 tablespoons of the mint. Pour in the stock. Bring the mixture to a boil, then add the potatoes. Lower the heat and simmer, partially covered, for about 20 minutes, or until the potatoes are tender.

2 Puree the mixture in a blender or food processor until smooth. Transfer to a clean pot or, if the soup is to be served cold, to a bowl. Season to taste with salt.

3 If the soup is to be served hot, add the cream and reheat it gently without boiling. Serve in warmed bowls, garnishing each portion with a little of the remaining chopped mint. If the soup is to be served cold, cover the bowl closely and chill for at least 3 hours. Just before serving, fold in the chilled cream. Serve in chilled bowls, garnished with the remaining chopped mint.

Roasted eggplant soup

serves **4–6**
preparation time **15 minutes**
cooking time **40–45 minutes**

2 lb eggplants
3 tablespoons olive oil
1 red onion
2 garlic cloves, crushed
5 cups Vegetable or Chicken Stock
  (see pages 8 and 9)
³/₄ cup crème fraîche or plain
  yogurt
2 tablespoons chopped mint
salt and pepper
mint sprigs, to garnish

1 Put the eggplants under a preheated hot broiler for about 20 minutes, turning occasionally, until the skin is well charred and the flesh has softened. Leave to cool slightly, then cut in half, scoop out the flesh, and chop.

2 Heat the oil in a pot over a low heat. Add the onion and garlic, and cook gently, without coloring, for 5–6 minutes, or until softened. Add the chopped eggplant and the stock, and cook for 10–15 minutes.

3 Puree the soup in a blender or food processor. Strain through a sieve and return to the pot to reheat. Season to taste with salt and pepper.

4 Mix the crème fraîche or plain yogurt with the chopped mint, and season to taste. Serve the soup in warmed bowls with a spoonful of the minted cream, garnishing each portion with mint sprigs.

Bortsch

serves **6**
preparation time **15 minutes**
cooking time **about 1½ hours**

4 raw beets
4 tomatoes, peeled and chopped
5 cups Vegetable or Beef Stock
   (see pages 8 and 11)
3 large cabbage leaves, coarsely
   shredded
1 bay leaf
½ teaspoon caraway seeds
6 black peppercorns, crushed
5 tablespoons red wine vinegar
2 tablespoons sugar
6 small potatoes
salt
6 teaspoons sour cream,
   to garnish

1 Put the beets into a pot. Cover with plenty of cold water and add 1 tablespoon salt. Bring to a boil, then lower the heat, cover, and simmer for 35–45 minutes. Drain, discarding the liquid, then rinse the beets under cold water, dry with paper towels, and slip off the skins.

2 Grate the beets into a large pot. Add the tomatoes, stock, cabbage leaves, bay leaf, caraway seeds, peppercorns, vinegar, sugar, and 2 teaspoons salt. Stir well. Bring the mixture to a boil, then lower the heat, cover and simmer gently for about 30 minutes.

3 Remove and discard the bay leaf. Drop the potatoes into the soup and continue simmering until the potatoes are tender but not too soft. Serve the soup hot in warmed bowls, garnishing each portion with a teaspoon of sour cream.

Caldo verde

serves **6**
preparation time **15 minutes**
cooking time **40 minutes**

2 tablespoons olive oil
1 large onion, chopped
2 garlic cloves, chopped
1 lb potatoes, cut into 1 inch
   cubes
5 cups water or Vegetable Stock
   (see page 8)
½ lb spring greens, finely shredded
2 tablespoons chopped parsley
salt and pepper
croutons, to serve (see page 18),
   made with strips of bread
   instead of cubes

1 Heat the oil in a large frying pan. Add the onion and cook for 5 minutes, or until softened but not brown. Add the garlic and potatoes, and cook for a few minutes, stirring occasionally.

2 Transfer the vegetables to a large pot. Add the water or stock, season to taste with salt and pepper, and cook for 15 minutes until the potatoes are tender.

3 Mash the potatoes roughly in their liquid, then add the spring greens and boil, uncovered, for 10 minutes.

4 Add the parsley and simmer for 2–3 minutes, or until heated through. Serve the soup in warmed bowls with croutons.

Gazpacho

serves **6**
preparation time **10–15 minutes**, plus chilling

2 garlic cloves, roughly chopped
¼ teaspoon salt
3 thick slices of white bread, crusts removed
2 lb tomatoes, peeled and roughly chopped
2 onions, roughly chopped
½ large cucumber, peeled, seeded and roughly chopped
2 large green bell peppers, cored, seeded and roughly chopped
5 tablespoons olive oil
4 tablespoons white wine vinegar
4 cups water
freshly ground black pepper

1 Combine the garlic and salt in a mortar, and pound with a pestle until it is smooth. Put the bread into a bowl and cover it with cold water. Soak for 5 seconds, then drain the bread, squeezing out the moisture.

2 Set aside a quarter of the tomatoes, onions, cucumber, and green peppers for the garnish. Put the remaining vegetables into a blender or food processor. Add the garlic paste, bread, and oil, and puree the mixture until smooth.

3 Pour the mixture into a bowl and stir in the vinegar and the measured water with pepper to taste. Cover closely and chill in the refrigerator for at least 3 hours.

4 Chop the reserved vegetables very finely and serve them separately in small bowls with the soup. Serve the soup very cold in chilled bowls.

Iced tomato and pepper soup with salsa verde

serves **4–6**

preparation time **about 30 minutes**, plus chilling

2 lb vine-ripened tomatoes, cored
2 large red bell peppers, cored, seeded, and roughly chopped
2 garlic cloves, chopped
1 small red chili, seeded and finely chopped
2½ cups Mediterranean tomato juice or passata (sieved tomatoes)
6 tablespoons olive oil
2 tablespoons balsamic vinegar
salt and pepper
2½ cups crushed ice, to serve

Salsa verde
2 garlic cloves, finely chopped
4 anchovy fillets in oil, rinsed and chopped
3 tablespoons each chopped parsley, mint, and basil
2 tablespoons salted capers, rinsed and chopped
⅔ cup olive oil, plus extra to seal
2 tablespoons lemon juice

1 Plunge the tomatoes into boiling water for 5–10 seconds, then remove them and refresh in cold water. Peel off the skins. Cut them in half around the middle and gently squeeze out and discard the seeds. Put the tomatoes into a blender or food processor.

2 Add the red peppers to the tomatoes with the garlic and chili and blend to a rough puree. Transfer to a bowl and stir in the tomato juice or passata, oil, and balsamic vinegar. Season with salt and pepper to taste, then cover and chill overnight in the refrigerator.

3 To make the salsa verde, pound 1 teaspoon salt with the garlic until creamy, using a mortar and pestle. Tip it into a bowl, and stir in the anchovies, herbs, capers, oil, lemon juice, and pepper to taste.

4 Stir the crushed ice into the soup and serve with the salsa verde in a separate bowl to stir into the soup.

Steamboat soup

serves **4–6**
preparation time **about
40 minutes**
cooking time **about 10 minutes**

8 tablespoons vegetable oil
10 garlic cloves, thinly sliced
1 tablespoon tamarind pulp
$^2/_3$ cup boiling water
5 cups water
2 tablespoons Thai fish sauce
1 teaspoon superfine sugar
1 small pineapple, peeled, cored
   and cut into chunks
2 medium tomatoes, quartered
8 scallions, finely sliced
$^1/_2$ lb raw jumbo shrimp
3 squid, cleaned and cut into
   thick rings
$^1/_2$ lb rainbow trout fillets, cut
   into pieces

To serve
handful of fresh cilantro leaves
handful of basil leaves
2 large chilies, diagonally sliced

1 Heat the oil in a small pot. When it is hot, deep-fry the garlic, a few slices at a time, until golden brown. Remove the garlic and drain on paper towels.

2 Put the tamarind pulp into a bowl with the measured boiling water, and set aside for 20 minutes to soften and dissolve. Strain the liquid through a sieve (discarding the pods and tamarind pits) and put into a pot with the measured water, fish sauce, sugar, pineapple, tomatoes, and scallions. Slowly bring to a boil.

3 If you are using a steamboat, pour the flavored stock into the hot pan containing smoking coals, and add the jumbo shrimp, squid rings, and pieces of fish. Simmer gently for 6–8 minutes. Alternatively, pour the hot stock into a large heavy-based pot, add the seafood and fish, and simmer gently for 6–8 minutes, or until cooked and tender.

4 Serve the steamboat while the fish is still cooking, topped with cilantro and basil leaves, slices of chili and the deep-fried garlic.

Miso soup with tofu

serves **4**
preparation time **10 minutes**
cooking time **35–40 minutes**

2 tablespoons red or white miso
1 small leek, cut into fine julienne
   strips
1/2 cup firm tofu, cut into small
   squares
1 tablespoon wakame seaweed

Dashi stock
1 tablespoon kombu seaweed
2 quarts water
2 tablespoons dried tuna
   (bonito) flakes
chives, to serve

1 First make the dashi stock. Wipe the kombu seaweed with a damp cloth and put it into a pot with the measured water. Bring to a simmer, skimming off any scum that rises to the surface with a slotted spoon. When the soup is clear, add 1 1/2 tablespoons of the dried tuna flakes, and simmer, uncovered, for 20 minutes. Remove the pan from the heat, and add the remaining dried tuna flakes. Set aside for 5 minutes, then strain the dashi, and return it to the pan.

2 Mix the miso with a little of the warm stock, then add 1 tablespoon at a time to the stock, stirring all the time until the miso has dissolved. Remove from the heat until ready to serve.

3 Warm the miso soup and add the leek and tofu with the wakame seaweed.

4 To serve, blanch the chives, tie them into a bundle, and float them on the top of the soup; then serve immediately in warmed bowls.

Mussel soup with saffron, basil, and spinach

serves **4**
preparation time **30 minutes**
cooking time **about 20 minutes**

pinch of saffron threads
$^1/_2$ cup boiling water
1$^1/_2$ lb live mussels, scrubbed
    and debearded
$^3/_4$ cup dry white wine
2 tablespoons olive oil
2 shallots, finely chopped
1 garlic clove, finely chopped
$^3/_4$ cup heavy cream
$^1/_4$–$^1/_2$ lb young leaf spinach,
    trimmed
15 basil leaves, shredded

1 Put the saffron into a small heatproof bowl, pour over the measured boiling water, and set aside to infuse. Discard any mussels that are broken or open. Put a large colander over another bowl.

2 Pour the wine into a pot large enough to accommodate all the mussels. Bring the wine to a boil and add the mussels. Cover with a tight-fitting lid and cook, shaking the pan frequently, for 2–3 minutes, or until the mussels have opened.

3 Tip the mussels into the colander and remove from their shells, discarding any that have not opened. Strain the mussel liquid through a muslin-lined sieve and set aside.

4 Heat the oil in a pot over a low heat. Add the shallots and garlic and cook gently, without coloring, for 5–6 minutes, or until softened. Add the strained mussel liquid, cream, and saffron and its infused liquid and bring to a boil. Lower the heat and add the spinach, half the basil, and all the mussels. Simmer for 2 minutes, then remove from the heat, stir in the remaining basil, and serve in warmed soup bowls.

Mediterranean salmon soup with rouille

serves **6**
preparation time **25 minutes**
cooking time **30 minutes**

1 tablespoon olive oil
1$\frac{1}{2}$ tablespoons butter
1 onion, finely chopped
1 carrot, finely diced
1 potato, no more than 7 oz, diced
1 garlic clove, finely chopped
1 teaspoon paprika, plus extra
  to garnish
2 large pinches of saffron threads
2 tomatoes, peeled and diced
1 tablespoon tomato paste
3$\frac{3}{4}$ cups Fish Stock (see page 10)
$\frac{1}{2}$ cup dry white wine
2 salmon steaks, about 7 oz each
$\frac{2}{3}$ cup milk
$\frac{2}{3}$ cup light cream
salt and pepper

Rouille
1 large mild red chili, seeded and
  chopped
1 garlic clove, finely chopped
3 tablespoons mayonnaise
1 small baguette, cut into 12 slices
  and toasted

1 Heat the oil and butter in a large pot. Add the onion, and cook gently for 5 minutes, stirring occasionally, until softened. Add the carrot and potato, and cook for 5 minutes.

2 Stir in the garlic, paprika, saffron, and tomatoes, and cook for 1 minute. Add the tomato paste, stock, and wine. Lower the salmon steaks into the stock and season generously with salt and pepper. Bring the stock to a boil, then lower the heat, cover, and simmer for 10–12 minutes, or until the salmon flakes easily when pressed lightly with a knife.

3 Lift the salmon out of the pot. Flake it into pieces using a knife and fork, and discard the skin and bones. Reserve one quarter of the salmon for garnish, then return the rest to the pot, and stir in the milk and cream. Puree the soup in a blender or food processor until smooth. Taste and adjust the seasoning if needed and reheat without boiling.

4 To make the rouille, puree the chili, garlic, and mayonnaise with a little salt and pepper in a blender or food processor until smooth. Toast the bread lightly on both sides and top with tiny spoonfuls of rouille. Ladle the soup into warmed bowls, sprinkle in the reserved salmon flakes, and float the toasts on top. Sprinkle with paprika and serve immediately.

Lobster and corn chowder

serves **4**
preparation time **20 minutes**, plus
preparing the lobsters
cooking time **1 hour**

2 cooked lobsters, 1 1/2 lb each
2 tablespoons butter
1 onion, finely chopped
1 carrot, finely chopped
1 celery stick, finely chopped
1 thyme sprig
1 parsley sprig
2 bay leaves
4 cups water

Chowder

7 oz can corn, drained
2 tablespoons butter
1 small onion, chopped
1 small garlic clove, crushed
1/3 cup pancetta, cut into
   small strips
1 1/4 cups milk
1 1/4 cups light cream
2 lb potatoes, cut into 3/4 inch dice
cayenne pepper
4 tomatoes, peeled, seeded,
   and chopped
salt and pepper

1 Cut the lobsters in half lengthwise and remove and discard the grayish-green tomalley (the liver), the gills, and the intestinal vein running along the back. Smash the claws and remove the meat. Cut up the remaining meat. Put the shells into a thick plastic bag and smash into small pieces with a rolling pin.

2 Put the butter into a large pot and melt over a low heat. Add the onion, carrot, and celery, and cook for 8–10 minutes, or until soft.

3 Add the herbs, measured water, and pieces of lobster shell. Bring to a boil, then lower the heat and simmer for 30 minutes. Strain through a fine sieve.

4 To make the chowder, place two-thirds of the corn in a blender or food processor with the strained lobster broth and puree until smooth. Melt the butter in a large flameproof casserole, add the onion and garlic, and cook gently for 5 minutes.

5 Add the pancetta and cook until golden. Add the pureed corn mixture, milk, cream, potatoes, and remaining corn. Bring to a boil, then lower the heat and simmer for 10–15 minutes, or until the potatoes are tender.

6 Season to taste with cayenne, salt and pepper; then stir in the tomatoes and lobster meat. Heat through without boiling and serve in warmed soup bowls.

Hot and Spicy Soups

The robust flavors of a wealth of cuisines are featured in these exotic recipes—sweet and aromatic Middle Eastern; fragrant and zesty Asian; piquant and fruity Caribbean; and out-and-out fiery Mexican.

Roasted tomato and chili soup with black olive cream

serves **4–6**
preparation time **30 minutes**
cooking time **about 1¼ hours**

3 lb ripe tomatoes, preferably plum
6 tablespoons olive oil
1½ teaspoons sea salt
1 tablespoon superfine sugar
1 large red chili
3–4 shallots or 1 onion, chopped
1 garlic clove, crushed
2½ cups water
2–4 tablespoons lime juice
salt and pepper

Olive cream
½ cup pitted black olives
3 tablespoons crème fraîche

1 Cut the tomatoes in half lengthwise and, holding each half over a bowl, scoop out the seeds with a teaspoon. Reserve the tomato seeds and any juice.

2 Lightly grease a baking sheet with a little of the oil and lay the tomatoes on it, cut-side up. Sprinkle them with about 4 tablespoons of the remaining oil, the sea salt, and sugar. Add the chili and put the baking sheet in a preheated oven, 350°F, for 45–50 minutes. Remove the chili after 20 minutes, when it is well charred and blistered. When cool, peel, seed, and chop it roughly.

3 Meanwhile, to make the olive cream, chop the olives very finely, fold them into the crème fraîche, and season to taste with salt and pepper.

4 Heat the remaining oil in a pot over a moderate heat. Add the shallots or onion, and cook for 6–8 minutes, or until lightly golden and softened. Add the garlic and cook for 2 minutes.

5 Add the roasted tomatoes with any liquid from the baking sheet, the reserved seeds and juice, the chili and the measured water. Bring the soup to a boil, then lower the heat and simmer for 10–12 minutes.

6 Puree the soup in a blender or food processor. Strain through a sieve and return to the pan to reheat. Season to taste with salt, pepper, and lime juice. Serve the soup in warmed bowls with a spoonful of the olive cream in each bowl.

Split pea soup with chorizo

serves **6–8**
preparation time **15–20 minutes**,
plus soaking
cooking time **about 2 hours**

3 cups split yellow peas, soaked
   overnight in cold water to cover
2 tablespoons olive oil
3 chorizo sausages, thinly sliced
1 onion, chopped
2 garlic cloves, finely chopped
5 cups Chicken Stock (see page 9)
3¾ cups water
1 bay leaf
1 thyme sprig or ¼ teaspoon
   dried thyme
3 carrots, quartered lengthwise
   and thinly sliced
salt

1 Drain the soaked split peas in a colander, rinse under cold running water, and drain again.

2 Heat the oil in a large pot. Cook the chorizo sausages over a moderate heat, stirring, for 5 minutes. With a slotted spoon, transfer the slices to paper towels to drain. Pour off all but 1 tablespoon of the fat in the pot.

3 Add the onion and garlic to the pot, and cook over a moderate heat until softened. Add the drained split peas, stock, measured water, bay leaf, and thyme. Bring the mixture to a boil, skimming off the scum as it rises to the surface with a slotted spoon. Lower the heat and simmer, partially covered, for 1¼ hours. Stir the mixture occasionally.

4 Add the carrots and cook for 30 minutes, or until tender. Season to taste with salt. Remove and discard the bay leaf, add the reserved chorizo, and cook for 10 minutes. Serve in warmed soup bowls.

White bean soup with toasted garlic and chili

serves **6**
preparation time **35 minutes**,
plus soaking
cooking time **1–1¼ hours**

$1\frac{1}{3}$ cups dried white beans
(haricot, cannellini, etc.), soaked
overnight in cold water to cover
Vegetable or Chicken Stock (see
pages 8 and 9), or cold water,
to cover
handful of sage leaves
4 garlic cloves
$\frac{2}{3}$ cup olive oil
2 tablespoons chopped sage or
rosemary
good pinch of dried red pepper
flakes
salt and pepper
roughly chopped parsley, to garnish

1 Drain the beans and put them into a flameproof casserole. Cover with the stock or water to a depth of 2 inches above the beans, and push in the sage leaves. Bring the beans to a boil, then cover them tightly and bake in a preheated oven, 325°F, for 40-60 minutes, depending on their freshness. Leave them in their cooking liquid.

2 Meanwhile, finely chop half the garlic and thinly slice the remainder.

3 Put half the beans, the cooked sage, and all the liquid into a blender or food processor and blend until smooth. Pour the puree back into the casserole with the remaining beans. If the soup is thicker than liked, add extra water or stock to thin it.

4 Heat half the oil in a frying pan and add the chopped garlic. Cook gently until it is soft and golden, then add the chopped sage or rosemary and cook for 30 seconds. Stir the mixture into the soup and reheat until boiling. Simmer gently for 10 minutes. Taste and season well with salt and pepper. Pour into a warmed tureen or ladle into warmed soup bowls.

5 Cook the sliced garlic carefully in the remaining oil until golden (don't let it become too dark or it will be bitter), then stir in the red pepper flakes. Dip the base of the pan into cold water to stop the garlic cooking, then spoon the garlic and oil over the soup. Serve sprinkled with chopped parsley.

Harira

serves **8–10**

preparation time **about 25 minutes**, plus soaking

cooking time **about 3 hours**

1¼ cups chickpeas, soaked for 48 hours in cold water to cover or 12 hours if covered with boiling water

2 chicken breasts, halved

5 cups Chicken Stock (see page 9)

5 cups water

2 x 14 oz cans chopped tomatoes

¼ teaspoon crumbled saffron threads

2 onions, chopped

⅔ cup long-grain white rice

⅓ cup green lentils, rinsed and drained

2 tablespoons finely chopped fresh cilantro

2 tablespoons finely chopped parsley

salt and pepper

1 Drain the chickpeas in a colander, rinse and drain again. Put them into a pot, cover with water to a depth of 2 inches above the chickpeas, and bring to a boil. Lower the heat and simmer, partially covered, for 2 hours, or until the chickpeas are tender, adding more water as necessary. Drain and set aside.

2 Put the chicken breasts, stock, and measured water in a separate pot. Bring to a boil, then lower the heat, cover and simmer for 10–15 minutes, or until the chicken is just cooked. Remove the chicken and shred it, discarding the skin and any bones. Set aside.

3 Add the chickpeas, tomatoes, saffron, onions, rice, and lentils to the stock in the pot. Simmer, covered, for 30–35 minutes, or until the rice and lentils are tender.

4 Add the shredded chicken, cilantro, and parsley, and heat for 5 minutes without boiling. Season with salt and pepper, and serve in warmed soup bowls.

Chili bean and pepper soup

serves **6**
preparation time **20 minutes**
cooking time **40 minutes**

2 tablespoons sunflower oil
1 large onion, finely chopped
4 garlic cloves, finely chopped
2 red bell peppers, cored, seeded,
    and diced
2 red chilies, seeded and finely
    chopped
3³/4 cups Vegetable Stock
    (see page 8)
3 cups tomato juice or passata
    (sieved tomatoes)
1 tablespoon double-concentrate
    tomato paste
1 tablespoon sun-dried tomato
    paste
2 tablespoons sweet chili sauce,
    or more to taste
13 oz can red kidney beans,
    drained
2 tablespoons finely chopped fresh
    cilantro
salt and pepper
lime rind strips, to garnish
    (optional)

To serve
¹/4 cup sour cream or crème fraîche
tortilla chips

1 Heat the oil in a large pot. Add the onion and garlic, and cook until soft but not colored. Stir in the red bell peppers and chilies, and fry for a few minutes. Stir in the stock and tomato juice or passata, tomato pastes, chili sauce, beans, and cilantro. Bring to a boil, then lower the heat, cover and simmer for 30 minutes.

2 Cool slightly, then puree in a blender or food processor until smooth. Return the soup to the pot and taste, adjusting the seasoning if necessary. Bring to a boil and serve in warmed soup bowls. Stir a little sour cream or crème fraîche into each portion and garnish with lime rind strips, if desired. Serve with tortilla chips.

Green lentil soup with spiced butter

serves **4**
preparation time **10 minutes**
cooking time **25–30 minutes**

2 tablespoons olive oil
2 onions, chopped
2 bay leaves
1 cup green lentils, rinsed and
    drained
4 cups Vegetable Stock
    (see page 8)
½ teaspoon ground turmeric
small handful of fresh cilantro
    leaves, roughly chopped
salt and pepper

Spiced butter
¼ cup lightly salted butter,
    softened
1 large garlic clove, crushed
1 tablespoon chopped fresh
    cilantro
1 teaspoon paprika
1 teaspoon cumin seeds
1 red chili, seeded and finely
    chopped

1 Heat the oil in a large pot. Add the onions and cook for 3 minutes. Add the bay leaves, lentils, stock, and turmeric. Bring to a boil, then lower the heat, cover and simmer for 20 minutes, or until the lentils are tender and turning mushy.

2 Meanwhile, to make the spiced butter, beat the butter with the garlic, cilantro, paprika, cumin, and chili. Transfer the mixture to a small serving dish.

3 Stir the cilantro leaves into the soup, season to taste with salt and pepper, and serve in warmed soup bowls with the spiced butter in a separate dish for stirring into the soup.

Red pepper and spicy chicken soup

serves **4**

preparation time **20 minutes**, plus cooling

cooking time **50 minutes**

3 red bell peppers, halved, cored and seeded

1 red onion, quartered

2 garlic cloves, unpeeled

2 teaspoons five-spice powder

5 oz boneless, skinless chicken breast

1 teaspoon olive oil

2 inch piece of fresh ginger root, grated

1 teaspoon ground cumin

1 teaspoon ground coriander

1 large potato, chopped

3$\frac{3}{4}$ cups Chicken Stock (see page 9)

salt and pepper

4 tablespoons fromage frais, to serve

1 Place the peppers, onion, and garlic cloves in a nonstick roasting pan. Roast in a preheated oven, 400°F, for 40 minutes, or until the peppers have blistered and the onion quarters and garlic are very soft. If the onion quarters start to brown too much, cover them with the pepper halves.

2 Meanwhile, scatter the five-spice powder over the chicken breast and broil under a medium heat for 20 minutes until crisp. When cooked, cut the chicken into thin shreds and put aside.

3 While the chicken is broiling, heat the oil in a pot and fry the ginger, cumin, and coriander over a low heat for 5 minutes, until softened. Add the potato and stir well. Season and pour in the chicken stock. Simmer, covered, for 30 minutes.

4 Remove the cooked vegetables from the oven. Place the peppers in a thick plastic bag. Tie the top and leave to cool. (The steam produced in the bag makes it easier to remove the skin when cool.) Add the onions to the potato mixture, and carefully squeeze out the garlic pulp into the pot, too. Peel the peppers and add to the soup. Simmer for 5 minutes.

5 Pour the soup into a blender or food processor and blend, in batches if necessary, for a few seconds until quite smooth. Return to the pot and thin with a little water, if necessary, to achieve the desired consistency. Stir the shredded chicken into the soup and simmer for 5 minutes.

6 Spoon into warmed bowls and top each one with a spoonful of fromage frais.

Spiced chickpea and lamb soup

serves **6**
preparation time **10 minutes**,
plus soaking
cooking time **2½ hours**

⅓ cup chickpeas, soaked overnight
    in cold water to cover
⅓ cup black-eyed peas, soaked
    overnight in cold water to cover
⅓ cup trahana or bulghur wheat
1 lb neck of lamb, cut into 4 pieces
4 tablespoons olive oil
1 onion, chopped
2 carrots, chopped
14 oz can chopped tomatoes
4 small red chilies
4 thyme sprigs
1 teaspoon each ground coriander,
    cumin, and cinnamon
½ teaspoon each dried mint and
    oregano
salt and pepper

To serve
olive oil
crusty bread

1 Drain the soaked peas and beans in a colander, rinse under cold running water, and drain again. Put them into separate pots, cover with plenty of cold water, and bring to a boil. Lower the heat and simmer for 1 hour, then drain and reserve the liquid.

2 Place the cooked pulses in a clay pot or casserole. Add all the remaining ingredients, and cover with the reserved liquid, adding extra water to cover, if necessary.

3 Cover the casserole with a tight-fitting lid and bake in a preheated oven, 350°F, for 1½ hours, or until the meat and vegetables are tender.

4 Serve each bowl of soup drizzled with olive oil and pass around some crusty bread.

Mexican soup with avocado salsa

serves **4**

preparation time **about 20 minutes**

cooking time **45 minutes**

2 tablespoons sunflower oil
1 large onion, chopped
2 garlic cloves, crushed
2 teaspoons ground coriander
1 teaspoon ground cumin
1 red bell pepper, cored, seeded, and diced
3 red chilies, seeded and sliced
14 oz can red kidney beans, drained and rinsed
3 cups tomato juice
1–2 tablespoons chili sauce
1/4 cup tortilla chips, crushed
salt and pepper
fresh cilantro sprigs, to garnish

Avocado salsa

1 small ripe avocado
4 scallions, finely chopped
1 tablespoon lemon juice
1 tablespoon chopped fresh cilantro
salt and pepper

1 Heat the oil in a large pot. Add the onion, garlic, spices, red pepper, and two-thirds of the chilies, and cook gently for 10 minutes. Add the beans, tomato juice, and chili sauce. Bring to a boil, then lower the heat, cover and simmer gently for 30 minutes.

2 Meanwhile, to make the avocado salsa, peel, pit, and finely dice the avocado. Put into a bowl and combine it with the scallions, lemon juice, and fresh cilantro. Season to taste with salt and pepper. Cover the bowl with plastic wrap, and set aside.

3 Puree the soup in a blender or food processor, together with the crushed tortilla chips. Return the soup to a clean pot, season with salt and pepper to taste, and heat through. Serve immediately in warmed soup bowls with the avocado salsa. Garnish with the reserved chili slices and the cilantro sprigs.

Jamaican pepperpot soup

serves **6–8**
preparation time **30–35 minutes**
cooking time **about 1¼ hours**

2 lb lean stewing beef, cut into
    small cubes
½ lb lean pork, cut into small
    cubes
2¾ quarts water
24 okra, conical stalk end
    discarded and roughly chopped
1 lb kale, roughly chopped
1 lb spinach, stems discarded and
    leaves roughly chopped
2 green bell peppers, cored, seeded,
    and roughly chopped
2 scallions, roughly chopped
1 fresh thyme sprig or ¼ teaspoon
    dried thyme
¼ teaspoon cayenne pepper
1 lb yellow yams, thinly sliced
1 large potato, thinly sliced
1 garlic clove, crushed or finely
    chopped
salt

1 Combine the meat with the measured water in a large pot. Bring to a boil, then lower the heat, and simmer the meat, partially covered, for about 30 minutes.

2 Add the okra, kale, spinach, green peppers, and scallions to the pot with the thyme and cayenne. Cook over a moderate heat, partially covered, for 15 minutes.

3 Add the yams, potato, and garlic to the pot, and cook for 20 minutes, or until the yams and potato are soft. Add more water if the soup is too thick. Season to taste with salt. Serve the soup hot in a warmed soup tureen.

Callaloo

serves **6**
preparation time **15 minutes**
cooking time **35 minutes**

3 tablespoons peanut oil
1 large onion, finely chopped
4 scallions, finely chopped
2 garlic cloves, crushed
1 red chili, seeded and finely
  chopped
1 teaspoon turmeric
1 thyme sprig, crumbled
1/2 lb okra, thinly sliced
1 lb fresh callaloo or spinach
  leaves, hard stems discarded and
  roughly chopped
3 3/4 cups Vegetable or Chicken
  Stock (see pages 8 and 9)
a few saffron threads
1 3/4 cups coconut milk
1/2 lb crab meat, fresh or canned
juice of 1/2 lime
dash of hot pepper sauce
salt and pepper

1 Heat the oil in a large pot. Add the onion, scallions, and garlic, and cook gently for 5 minutes, or until softened. Add the chili, turmeric, and thyme, and stir over a low heat for 1–2 minutes.

2 Stir in the okra, then add the callaloo or spinach leaves. Turn up the heat and cook, stirring, until the leaves start to wilt. Lower the heat and add the stock and saffron. Bring to a boil, then lower the heat, cover and simmer for 20 minutes.

3 Add the coconut milk and crab meat, and stir well. Heat gently for 4–5 minutes and then season to taste with salt and pepper. Just before serving, stir in the lime juice and hot pepper sauce.

Moroccan fish soup

serves **6–8**
preparation time **about 35 minutes**
cooking time **about 40 minutes**

3 tablespoons olive oil
2 onions, chopped
2 celery sticks, sliced
4 garlic cloves, crushed
1 red chili, seeded and chopped
½ teaspoon ground cumin
1 cinnamon stick
½ teaspoon ground coriander
2 large potatoes, chopped
6 cups Fish Stock (see page 10)
  or water
3 tablespoons lemon juice
4 lb mixed fish and shellfish,
  prepared
4 well-flavored tomatoes, peeled,
  seeded if desired, and chopped
1 large bunch of mixed dill,
  parsley, and fresh cilantro,
  chopped
salt and pepper

1 Heat the oil in a large pot. Add the onion and celery, and cook gently until softened and transparent, adding the garlic and chili toward the end. Add the cumin, cinnamon, and ground coriander, and stir for 1 minute; then add the potatoes and cook, stirring, for 2 minutes.

2 Add the stock or water and the lemon juice, and simmer gently, uncovered, for about 20 minutes, or until the potatoes are tender.

3 Add the fish and shellfish, the tomatoes, herbs, and salt and pepper to taste, and cook gently until the fish and shellfish are tender. Serve in warmed soup bowls.

tip Any selection of fish and shellfish can be used for fish soup, with the exception of oily fish such as mackerel and sardines. The trimmings, heads, tails, bones, and shells can be used to make the fish stock.

Wonton soup

serves **4**
preparation time **25 minutes**
cooking time **15 minutes**

20 wonton wrappers
5 cups Chicken Stock (see page 9)
2 pink Asian shallots or 1 small
   onion, finely chopped
1 inch piece of fresh ginger root,
   peeled and finely sliced
1 teaspoon superfine sugar
4 scallions, finely sliced
½ tablespoon light soy sauce
1 teaspoon rice vinegar
handful of roughly chopped parsley
1 teaspoon sesame oil
salt and pepper
chili oil, to serve

Filling
¼ lb white fish or shrimp
¼ lb white crab meat
2 scallions, finely chopped
1 inch piece of fresh ginger root,
   peeled and finely chopped
1 garlic clove, crushed

1 First make the filling. Chop the fish or shrimp and crab meat very finely with the scallions, chopped ginger, and garlic, or put all the ingredients in a blender or food processor and blend to a paste.

2 Put 1 teaspoon of the mixture on a wonton wrapper, brush around the filling with a little water, and fold the wrapper over to make a triangle. Repeat with the remaining mixture until all the wontons are made. Keep the wrappers covered with a damp cloth to prevent them from drying out before you fill them.

3 Put the stock into a pot with the shallots or small onion and sliced ginger, and bring to a boil. Lower the heat and add the sugar and filled wontons. Simmer gently for 5 minutes.

4 Add the scallions, soy sauce, vinegar, parsley, and salt and pepper to taste. Just before serving, add the sesame oil. Serve the soup in warmed bowls accompanied by small dishes of chili oil.

Hot and sour shrimp noodle soup

serves **4**
preparation time **20 minutes**,
plus soaking
cooking time **35–40 minutes**

1 lb raw large shrimp in their
  shells, defrosted if frozen
1 tablespoon sunflower oil
2 scallions, roughly chopped
1 inch piece of fresh ginger root,
  peeled and chopped
1 small red or green chili, seeded,
  and finely chopped
2 Kaffir lime leaves or rind from
  1 lime, cut into strips
2 lemon grass stalks, bruised and
  chopped into 1 inch pieces, or
  1 tablespoon dried chopped
  lemon grass, soaked in hot water
  to cover for 30 minutes
5 cups Chicken Stock (see page 9)
2–4 tablespoons lime juice
³/₄ cup fine egg or rice noodles
¹/₄ lb small oyster mushrooms

To garnish
2 scallions, cut into thin strips
fresh cilantro sprigs

1 Peel and devein the shrimp, reserving the shells.
Rinse the shrimp and set aside.

2 Heat the oil in a large pot. Add the chopped
scallions, ginger, and chili and cook gently, without
coloring, for 5 minutes. Add the reserved shrimp shells
and cook for 3 minutes, then add the lime leaves or
rind, lemon grass (if using dried lemon grass, add it
with its soaking liquid), stock, and 2 tablespoons lime
juice. Bring to a boil, then lower the heat and simmer
gently for 20 minutes.

3 Meanwhile, cook the noodles according to the
package instructions, drain and set aside.

4 Strain the stock through a fine sieve into a clean
pot. Taste and add more lime juice if required. Bring
back to a boil, then lower the heat, add the shrimp,
and cook for about 2 minutes, or until opaque. Add
the mushrooms and cook for 1–2 minutes, or until
just soft. Add the noodles and heat through. Serve in
warmed soup bowls, sprinkled with scallion strips and
cilantro sprigs.

Malaysian laksa

serves **4**
preparation time **15 minutes**
cooking time **25–30 minutes**

3 tablespoons peanut oil
2 large onions, finely chopped
4 garlic cloves, crushed
3 red bird's eye chilies, finely
  chopped
3/4 cup roasted peanuts, chopped
1 tablespoon ground coriander
1 tablespoon ground cumin
2 teaspoons turmeric
5 cups coconut milk
1 teaspoon shrimp paste
1–2 tablespoons sugar, to taste
3/4 lb cooked chicken, shredded
1 1/2 cups bean sprouts
1 lb fresh flat rice noodles
4 scallions, chopped
3 tablespoons chopped fresh
  cilantro leaves
salt and pepper

To serve
4 scallions, chopped
1 large red chili, finely sliced
1–2 tablespoons chopped roasted
  peanuts

1 Heat the oil in a saucepan, add the onions, and cook until golden brown. Add the garlic, chilies, peanuts, ground coriander, cumin, and turmeric. Cook for 2–3 minutes, or until the spices have cooked through and released a strong aroma.

2 Stir the coconut milk and shrimp paste into the spice mixture, cover and simmer for 15 minutes. Season the spiced coconut with salt, pepper, and sugar to taste. Add the shredded chicken and half the bean sprouts and simmer for 5 minutes.

3 Blanch the noodles in boiling water and divide between 4 large bowls. Sprinkle with the scallions and fresh cilantro, and divide the remaining raw bean sprouts between the bowls.

4 Ladle the chicken and coconut mixture over the noodles, and serve with scallions, red chili and roasted peanuts, in separate bowls for garnishing.

Beef and flat noodle soup

serves **4–6**
preparation time **25 minutes**
cooking time **2¼ hours**

1 lb chuck steak
2 quarts Beef Stock (see page 11)
    or water
4 star anise
1 large cinnamon stick
1 teaspoon black peppercorns
2 sweet onions or 4 shallots,
    thinly sliced
4 garlic cloves, crushed
3 inch piece of fresh ginger root,
    finely sliced
1 cup bean sprouts
1½ cups dried flat rice noodles
6 scallions, thinly sliced
handful of fresh cilantro leaves
½ lb filet mignon, thinly sliced
2 tablespoons fish sauce
salt and pepper
red bird's eye chilies, to garnish

Nuoc cham sauce
2 red chilies, chopped
1 garlic clove
1½ tablespoons superfine sugar
1 tablespoon lime juice
1 tablespoon rice vinegar
3 tablespoons fish sauce
4 tablespoons water

To serve
bean sprouts
thin scallions, sliced
1 large red chili, sliced

1 Heat a large dry frying pan until very hot and sear the chuck steak on all sides until brown and charred.

2 Put the beef into a large pot with the stock or water, star anise, cinnamon, black peppercorns, 1 sliced onion or 2 shallots, the garlic, and ginger. Bring to a boil, skimming off any scum that rises to the surface with a slotted spoon, and continue to boil for about 10 minutes. Lower the heat, cover and simmer for about 2 hours, or until the beef is tender.

3 Blanch the bean sprouts in boiling water for 1 minute.

4 Cook the noodles in boiling water for 3–4 minutes, or until just soft. Do not overcook them. Drain well and put into 4 large soup bowls. Arrange the bean sprouts, scallions, cilantro leaves, and the remaining onions or shallots over the noodles.

5 To make the nuoc cham sauce, pound the chopped chilies, garlic, and sugar until smooth, using a mortar and pestle. Add the lime juice, vinegar, fish sauce, and measured water, and blend together well. Put the mixture into a small bowl.

6 When the beef from the broth is tender, lift it out, slice it thinly, and divide it between the soup bowls with the slices of raw filet mignon. Garnish with the red bird's eye chilies.

7 Strain the broth, return it to the pot, and season to taste with fish sauce, salt and pepper. To serve, ladle the hot broth over the contents of the bowls and serve immediately with the nuoc cham sauce and a plate of extra bean sprouts, scallions and red chili.

Winter Warmers

The perfect meal-in-a-bowl, there is nothing more comforting and satisfying than soup. These hearty dishes are thick with root vegetables, pulses, and grains, and include delicious toppings, such as garlic croutons, grated cheese, or sour cream.

Cream of celeriac soup with bolete dumplings

serves **4–6**
preparation time **25 minutes**, plus soaking and chilling
cooking time **35–40 minutes**

¹/₄ cup butter
2 shallots or 1 onion, chopped
1 garlic clove, crushed
1 lb celeriac, cut into small dice
3³/₄ cups Vegetable or Chicken Stock (see pages 8 and 9)
1¹/₄ cups light cream or milk
salt and pepper
finely grated Parmesan cheese, to serve

Dumplings
1 tablespoon dried bolete mushrooms (ceps)
2 tablespoons butter
1 shallot, finely chopped
³/₄ cup ricotta cheese
¹/₄ cup finely grated Parmesan cheese
2 egg yolks, beaten
2 tablespoons all-purpose flour, plus extra for rolling
1 tablespoon chopped parsley

1 To make the dumplings, put the bolete into a small bowl and pour over warm water to cover. Leave to soak for 30 minutes. Drain in a fine sieve, reserving the liquid. Rinse the mushrooms well in cold water, chop finely, and set aside.

2 Melt the butter in a small saucepan over a low heat, add the shallot, and cook gently, without coloring, for 5–6 minutes, or until softened. Spoon into a bowl, add the remaining ingredients, and mix to form a soft dough. Season to taste with salt and pepper. Cover and chill for 30–60 minutes. With lightly floured hands, form the mixture into about 30 small balls, roll in flour, and put onto a tray.

3 Meanwhile, to make the soup, melt the butter in a pot over a moderate heat, add the shallots or onion and garlic, and cook, without coloring, for 5 minutes. Add the celeriac, cover, and cook for 5–10 minutes, or until the celeriac begins to soften. Add the stock and bring to a boil, then lower the heat, and simmer for 10–15 minutes.

4 Puree the soup in a blender or food processor until smooth. Return the soup to the pan, stir in the cream or milk, and season to taste. Reheat without boiling.

5 Bring a pot of lightly salted water to a boil. Add the dumplings and simmer for 3–4 minutes. Drain well and add to the soup just before serving. Serve in warmed soup bowls, sprinkled with grated Parmesan.

Chestnut soup

serves **6**

preparation time **20 minutes**, plus soaking (if using dried chestnuts)

cooking time **45 minutes–1 hour**

1½ lb fresh, plump, sweet chestnuts or ¾ lb dried chestnuts, soaked overnight in cold water to cover

½ cup butter

1 cup chopped pancetta or streaky bacon

2 onions, finely chopped

1 carrot, chopped

1 celery stick, chopped

2 garlic cloves, halved

1 tablespoon chopped rosemary

2 bay leaves

salt and pepper

rosemary sprigs, to garnish

1 If you are using fresh chestnuts, use a small sharp knife to slit the shell of each chestnut across the rounded side. Put them into a pot and cover with cold water. Bring to a boil, then lower the heat, and simmer for 15–20 minutes. Lift out the chestnuts and discard the water. Peel off the thick outer skin and the thinner inner skin, which has a bitter taste.

2 Melt the butter in a large pot and add the pancetta or bacon. Cook over a moderate heat until beginning to turn golden. Add the onions, carrot, and celery and cook for 5–10 minutes, or until softened.

3 Add the chestnuts to the pot (including the soaking water from dried chestnuts) with the garlic, rosemary, bay leaves, and enough water to cover completely. Bring to a boil, then simmer for 30 minutes, stirring occasionally. Season with salt and pepper. Serve in warmed bowls, garnished with rosemary.

Sweet potato soup

serves **6–8**
preparation time **15 minutes**
cooking time **50 minutes–1 hour**

4–6 rindless smoked bacon slices
2 tablespoons butter
1 onion, chopped
2 carrots, sliced
2 celery sticks, sliced
1 bay leaf
1½ lb sweet potatoes, sliced
½ lb potatoes, sliced
5 cups Chicken Stock (see page 9)
⅔ cup water
½ cup dry white wine
¼ teaspoon grated nutmeg
¼ teaspoon white pepper
salt

1 Heat the bacon in a frying pan over a gentle heat until the fat runs; then raise the heat and cook over a moderate heat until very crisp. Using tongs, transfer the bacon onto paper towels to drain.

2 Add the butter to the bacon fat left in the frying pan, and cook the onion, carrots, celery, and bay leaf over a low heat for 5–8 minutes, stirring frequently.

3 Transfer the mixture to a pot. Add the sweet potatoes, potatoes, stock, measured water, and wine. Bring the mixture to a boil, then lower the heat and simmer, covered, for 35–40 minutes, or until the vegetables are very tender. Remove and discard the bay leaf.

4 Puree the mixture in a blender or food processor until smooth. Transfer to a clean saucepan. Add the nutmeg, white pepper, and salt to taste. Put the pan over a moderate heat, stirring, until the soup is hot.

5 Serve the soup in warmed bowls, garnishing each portion with the reserved bacon.

Tomato and bread soup

serves **4**

preparation time **10 minutes**

cooking time **about 35 minutes**

2 lb vine-ripened tomatoes, peeled,
seeded, and chopped

1¼ cups Vegetable Stock
(see page 8)

6 tablespoons olive oil

2 garlic cloves, crushed

1 teaspoon sugar

2 tablespoons chopped basil

4 slices day-old bread, without
crusts

1 tablespoon balsamic vinegar

salt and pepper

pesto, to serve (optional)

1 Put the tomatoes into a pot with the stock,
2 tablespoons of the oil, the garlic, sugar, and basil,
and bring gradually to a boil. Lower the heat, cover
and simmer gently for 30 minutes.

2 Crumble the bread into the soup and stir over a low
heat until it has thickened. Stir in the balsamic vinegar
and the remaining oil, and season to taste with salt
and pepper. Stir a spoonful of pesto into each bowl
before serving, if liked.

Kale soup with garlic croutons

serves **8–10**
preparation time **20–25 minutes**
cooking time **about 45 minutes**

¼ cup butter
1 onion, chopped
2 carrots, sliced
1 lb kale, thick stems discarded
5 cups water
2½ cups Vegetable Stock
    (see page 8)
1 tablespoon lemon juice
4–5 medium potatoes, sliced
pinch of grated nutmeg
salt and pepper
2 kale leaves, finely shredded,
    to garnish
garlic croutons, to serve
    (see below)

1 Melt the butter in a large pot. Add the onion and cook over a moderate heat until soft but not brown, stirring frequently. Add the carrots and kale in batches, stirring constantly. Cook for 2 minutes. Add the measured water, stock, lemon juice, potatoes, nutmeg, and salt and pepper to taste. Bring to a boil, stirring from time to time. Lower the heat, cover and simmer for 30–35 minutes, or until all the vegetables are soft.

2 Puree the mixture in a blender or food processor until smooth. Transfer to a clean pot. If the soup is too thick, add some water.

3 Add the shredded kale leaves to the pan and cook, stirring constantly, until crisp.

4 Check the seasoning and reheat the soup without boiling. Serve in warmed soup bowls with the garlic croutons and garnish with the crisp kale.

tip To make garlic croutons, cut the crusts off 2 slices of white bread and gently rub the bread all over with the cut sides of a halved garlic clove, then cube the bread. Heat 1 tablespoon vegetable oil in a heavy-based frying pan and fry the bread cubes, turning and stirring frequently, for 1–2 minutes, or until golden and crisp.

Pumpkin and apple soup

serves **4–5**
preparation time **15 minutes**
cooking time **30 minutes**

2 tablespoons butter
1 large onion, roughly chopped
2 teaspoons chopped fresh thyme
2 small cooking apples, peeled,
  cored, and roughly chopped
3 tablespoons dark soft brown
  sugar
2 tablespoons whole-grain
  mustard
1 small pumpkin, about 1½ lb,
  peeled, seeded, and cut into
  chunks
4 cups Vegetable Stock
  (see page 8)
½ cup crème fraîche
salt and pepper
pumpkin seeds, to serve

1 Melt the butter in a large pot. Add the onion and thyme, and cook gently, stirring frequently, for about 5 minutes, or until softened and beginning to color. Add the apples and sugar and cook gently for 3 minutes.

2 Add the mustard, pumpkin, and stock, and bring just to a boil. Lower the heat, cover and simmer gently for about 20 minutes, or until the pumpkin and apples are very soft and falling apart.

3 Puree the mixture in a blender or food processor until smooth.

4 Stir in half the crème fraîche, season to taste with salt and pepper, and heat through gently. Ladle into warmed soup bowls, spoon over the remaining crème fraîche and serve sprinkled with pumpkin seeds

Oven-baked vegetable soup

serves **4**
preparation time **15 minutes**
cooking time **about 1¼ hours**

1 onion, roughly chopped
2 garlic cloves, chopped
2 large carrots, thinly sliced
1 leek, thickly sliced
1 large parsnip, diced
1⅓ cups diced rutabaga
4 tablespoons olive oil
2 teaspoons clear honey
4 thyme sprigs
4 rosemary sprigs
2 bay leaves
4 ripe tomatoes, quartered
5 cups Vegetable Stock
  (see page 8)
salt and pepper
buttered toast, to serve

1 Toss the vegetables with the oil and honey and put into a roasting pan. Add the herbs and transfer to a preheated oven, 400°F. Roast for about 50–60 minutes, or until all the vegetables are golden and tender. Add the tomatoes halfway through cooking. Lower the oven temperature to 375°F.

2 Remove and discard the herbs, and transfer the vegetables to a blender or food processor. Add half the stock and process until smooth, then blend in the remaining stock.

3 Transfer the soup to a casserole. Season to taste with salt and pepper and bake for 20 minutes, or until heated through. Serve in warmed soup bowls with buttered toast.

Country bean and vegetable broth

serves **4**
preparation time **10 minutes**,
plus soaking
cooking time **about 1¼ hours**

¼ cup each dried kidney beans,
   pinto beans, and black-eyed
   peas, soaked overnight in cold
   water to cover, drained,
   and rinsed
2 tablespoons dried bolete
   mushrooms (ceps)
1 tablespoon olive oil
2 shallots, finely chopped
2 garlic cloves, crushed
¼ lb button mushrooms, diced
2 tablespoons chopped mixed fresh
   herbs, plus extra to garnish
½ cup mini pasta shapes
5 cups hot Beef Stock
   (see page 11)
salt and pepper

1 Put the beans into a large pot with water to cover. Bring to a boil and boil vigorously for 10 minutes. Skim any scum that rises to the surface of the liquid with a slotted spoon and lower the heat. Simmer, covered, for 1 hour, or until all the beans are very tender.

2 Meanwhile, put the dried mushrooms into a heatproof bowl, cover with boiling water, and set aside for 15 minutes; then drain and reserve the liquid.

3 Heat the oil in a large pot, add the shallots and garlic, and cook for 3 minutes. Add the fresh mushrooms and stir well. Add the herbs and pasta shapes. Drain the beans and add them to the pot with the hot stock, reserved mushroom liquid, and salt and pepper to taste. Bring to a boil, then lower the heat, and simmer for about 12 minutes. Serve immediately in warmed bowls, sprinkled with chopped herbs to garnish.

Tasty bean soup

serves **4**

preparation time **30 minutes**,
plus soaking

cooking time **about 2¼ hours**

2 cups dried haricot beans, soaked
    overnight in cold water to cover
2¼ quarts water
1 carrot, chopped
1 onion, quartered
1 bouquet garni
¼ lb cooked smoked ham, diced
2½ tablespoons butter
2 shallots, finely chopped
1 garlic clove, crushed
1 tablespoon chopped parsley
salt and pepper
parsley sprigs, to garnish
1 cup croutons, to serve
    (see page 18)

1 Drain the beans in a colander, rinse under cold running water, and drain again.

2 Put the beans into a large pot with the measured water and bring to a boil over a moderate heat. Boil for 1½ hours, or until the beans are just tender. Add the carrot, onion, bouquet garni, and ham, and simmer for 20–30 minutes. Remove and discard the bouquet garni. Puree the soup in a blender or food processor until smooth. Return to the pot and reheat over a moderate heat.

3 Melt the butter in a heavy-based pot, add the shallots and garlic, and cook gently until golden but not brown. Add the parsley and mix together quickly. Add the shallot mixture to the bean Puree.

4 Mix well with a wooden spoon. Season well with salt and pepper, then pour into warmed soup bowls. Sprinkle with croutons and garnish with parsley sprigs.

Goulash soup

serves **6–8**
preparation time **10–15 minutes**
cooking time **1¼ hours**

3 tablespoons vegetable oil
1½ lb boneless lean beef, cut into
   1 inch strips
2 onions, chopped
2 garlic cloves, crushed
2 celery stalks, sliced
3 tablespoons paprika
1 tablespoon caraway seeds
5 cups Beef Stock (see page 11)
2½ cups water
¼ teaspoon dried thyme
2 bay leaves
¼ teaspoon Tabasco sauce,
   or to taste
3 tablespoons tomato paste
½ lb potatoes, cut into ½ inch dice
3 carrots, cut into ½ inch dice
6–8 teaspoons sour cream,
   to garnish (optional)

1 Heat the oil in a large pot and brown the meat in batches over a moderate heat. As each batch browns, transfer it to paper towels to drain. Add the onions, garlic, and celery to the remaining oil, and cook until transparent.

2 Take the pan off the heat and stir in the paprika, caraway seeds, stock, and the measured water. Add the thyme, bay leaves, Tabasco, and tomato paste. Stir well and add the cooked beef. Bring the mixture to a boil, then lower the heat and simmer, partially covered, for 30 minutes.

3 Add the diced potatoes and carrots, then simmer for 30 minutes, or until the potatoes are tender. Remove and discard the bay leaves. Serve the soup immediately in warmed bowls, garnishing each portion with a teaspoon of sour cream, if desired.

Spanish chickpea soup

serves **8–10**
preparation time **15 minutes**,
plus soaking
cooking time **2½–2¾ hours**

¾ cup dried chickpeas, soaked for
   48 hours in cold water to cover
   or 12 hours if covered with
   boiling water
1 small smoked, boneless bacon
   hock joint, about 1–1½ lb
1 onion, studded with 4 cloves
2 garlic cloves, crushed
1 bay leaf
1 thyme sprig or ¼ teaspoon
   dried thyme
1 marjoram sprig or ½ teaspoon
   dried marjoram
1 parsley sprig
2 quarts water
2 quarts Chicken Stock
   (see page 9)
6–7 medium potatoes, cut into
   ½ inch dice
½ lb Savoy cabbage, shredded
salt and pepper

1 Drain the chickpeas in a colander, rinse under cold running water, and drain again. Put the bacon joint into a deep pot and cover with cold water. Bring the water briefly to a boil, then drain, discarding the water.

2 Return the bacon joint to the clean pot. Add the chickpeas, onion, garlic, bay leaf, thyme, marjoram, parsley, and the measured water. Bring the mixture to a boil, then lower the heat and simmer, partially covered, for 1½ hours. Remove and discard the onion, bay leaf, and thyme, marjoram, and parsley sprigs. Lift out the hock, put it on a board, and cut it into small pieces. Set the pieces aside.

3 Add the stock, potatoes, and cabbage to the pan and simmer for 30 minutes. Add the reserved hock pieces to the soup and cook for 10 minutes. Season to taste with salt and pepper. Serve in warmed soup bowls.

La Ribollita

serves **8**
preparation time **30 minutes**,
plus soaking and chilling
cooking time **about 3 hours**

²/₃ cup olive oil
1 onion, finely chopped
1 carrot, chopped
1 celery stalk, chopped
2 leeks, finely chopped
4 garlic cloves, finely chopped
1 small white cabbage, shredded
1 large potato, chopped
4 zucchini, chopped
1¼ cups dried cannellini beans,
   soaked overnight in cold water
   to cover, drained and rinsed
1³/₄ cups passata (sieved tomatoes)
2 rosemary sprigs
2 thyme sprigs
2 sage sprigs
1 dried red chili
4½ pints water
1 lb cavolo nero (Tuscan black
   cabbage) or Savoy cabbage,
   finely shredded
6 thick slices of coarse crusty
   white bread
1 garlic clove, bruised
salt and pepper

To serve
olive oil
freshly grated Parmesan cheese

1 Heat half the oil in a large pot and add the onion, carrot, and celery. Cook gently for about 10 minutes, stirring frequently. Add the leeks and finely chopped garlic, and cook for 10 minutes. Add the white cabbage, potato, and zucchini, stir well and cook for 10 minutes, stirring frequently.

2 Stir in the soaked beans, passata, rosemary, thyme, sage, dried chili, salt to taste, and plenty of black pepper. Cover with the measured water (the vegetables should be well covered) and bring to a boil, then lower the heat and simmer, covered, for at least 2 hours, or until the beans are very soft.

3 Remove 2–3 ladlefuls of soup, mash it well, then return to the pan. Stir in the cavolo nero or Savoy cabbage and simmer for 15 minutes. Leave the soup to cool, then cover and refrigerate overnight.

4 The next day, slowly reheat the soup, season if necessary, and stir in the remaining oil. Toast the bread and rub it with the bruised garlic. Arrange the bread over the base of a tureen or in individual bowls and ladle the soup over it. Drizzle with oil and serve with plenty of freshly grated Parmesan.

Risi e bisi with frazzled prosciutto

serves **4**
preparation time **10 minutes**
cooking time **20–30 minutes**,
plus **5–10 minutes** for fresh peas

3 tablespoons olive oil
1 onion, chopped
5 cups Chicken Stock (see page 9)
1 cup risotto rice
1½ lb fresh young peas in the pod,
    shelled, or ½ lb frozen peas,
    defrosted
large pinch of sugar
4 slices of prosciutto
2 tablespoons chopped Italian
    parsley
½ cup Parmesan cheese, finely
    grated, plus extra to serve
salt and pepper

1 Heat 2 tablespoons of the oil in a large pot. Add the onion and cook, without coloring, for 5–10 minutes, or until softened.

2 Add the stock and bring to a boil, then lower the heat and stir in the rice. (If using fresh peas, add them now and simmer gently for 5 minutes before adding the rice.) Season with salt and pepper and add the sugar. Cover and simmer gently, stirring occasionally, for 15–20 minutes, or until the rice is just tender. (If using frozen peas, add them after 10–15 minutes.)

3 Cut each slice of prosciutto in half lengthwise. Heat the remaining oil in a large frying pan, add the prosciutto strips and cook over a high heat for 10–15 seconds, or until crisp. Drain on paper towels.

4 Stir the parsley and grated Parmesan into the soup. Serve in warmed soup bowls, topped with 2 pieces of the frazzled prosciutto and some grated Parmesan.

Barley soup with pork and cabbage

serves **6**
preparation time **15 minutes**
cooking time **55 minutes**

4 tablespoons olive oil
1 garlic clove, chopped
1 onion, chopped
5 cups Beef Stock (see page 11)
3 cups water
10 oz lean pork, cut into
  ³/₄ inch strips
2 carrots, chopped
¹/₂–³/₄ lb spring or savoy cabbage,
  roughly chopped
³/₄ cup barley
¹/₂–³/₄ lb potatoes, cut into
  ¹/₂ inch dice
salt and pepper

1 Heat the oil in a large pot, add the garlic and onion, and cook over a moderate heat until softened.

2 Add the stock, the measured water, pork, carrots, cabbage, and barley. Bring the mixture to a boil, then lower the heat, cover and simmer for 20 minutes.

3 Add the potatoes with salt and pepper to taste. If the soup is too thick, add a little water. Replace the lid and simmer for 30 minutes. Stir from time to time. Serve in warmed soup bowls.

Gruyère soup with bacon and potatoes

serves **6–8**
preparation time **20 minutes**
cooking time **about 25 minutes**

2 tablespoons olive oil
3 slices rindless smoked bacon,
   chopped
2 onions, finely chopped
2$^1/_2$ cups Chicken Stock
   (see page 9)
3$^3/_4$ cups water
1$^1/_4$ lb potatoes, cut into
   $^1/_2$ inch dice
4 tablespoons all-purpose flour
$^1/_2$ cup Gruyère cheese, grated
1 tablespoon medium dry sherry
1 teaspoon Worcestershire sauce
3 tablespoons finely chopped
   parsley
salt and pepper

1 Heat the oil in a large pot. Add the bacon and onions, and cook over a moderate heat until the onion is pale golden. Add the stock, 2$^1/_2$ cups of the measured water and the potatoes. Bring the mixture to a boil, then lower the heat, cover and simmer, for 15 minutes, or until the potatoes are just tender.

2 In a small bowl, whisk the flour with the remaining water and stir it into the soup. Cook, covered, for 5 minutes, stirring frequently.

3 Blend the Gruyère with 1$^1/_4$ cups of the soup in a blender or food processor. Stir the Puree back into the soup, then add the sherry and Worcestershire sauce with salt and pepper to taste. Simmer for 3–5 minutes, then stir in the parsley just before serving in warmed soup bowls.

Smoked haddock and corn soup with wild rice and bacon croutons

serves **4**
preparation time **15 minutes**
cooking time **about 1¼ hours**

⅓ cup wild rice
½ lb smoked haddock
2½ cups milk
1 bay leaf
¼ cup butter
1 large onion, chopped
1 leek, sliced
1 celery stalk, chopped
1 garlic clove, crushed
1 tablespoon thyme leaves
3¾ cups Chicken Stock
   (see page 9)
pinch of grated nutmeg
¾ cup corn, defrosted if frozen
salt and pepper
2 tablespoons chopped parsley,
   to serve

Bacon croutons
3 tablespoons olive oil
4 rindless pancetta or streaky
   bacon slices, cut into strips
2 slices of bread, crusts removed,
   cut or broken into ½ inch pieces

1 Put the rice into a small saucepan and cover with cold water. Bring to a boil, then lower the heat and simmer for 40–45 minutes, or until tender. Drain and set aside.

2 Put the haddock, milk, and bay leaf into a saucepan and bring to a boil, then lower the heat and simmer for 8–10 minutes, or until just cooked. Remove the fish with a slotted spoon and leave to cool. Discard the skin and any bones and break the flesh into flakes with a fork. Strain the milk and reserve it.

3 Melt the butter in a large pot. Add the onion, leek, celery, and garlic, and cook, without coloring, for 8–10 minutes. Add the thyme, stock, and reserved milk. Season with salt, pepper, and nutmeg. Bring to a boil, then lower the heat and simmer for 10 minutes. Add the corn and cook for 5 minutes, then add the rice and flaked haddock, and heat for a few minutes. Adjust the seasoning to taste.

4 To make the bacon croutons, heat the oil in a large frying pan over a moderate heat. Add the pancetta or bacon and cook for 5–6 minutes, or until crisp.

5 Remove with a slotted spoon and drain on paper towels. Add the bread to the pan and cook for 4–5 minutes, turning frequently, until crisp and golden brown. Drain on paper towels.

6 Serve the soup in warmed soup bowls, sprinkled with the bacon croutons and chopped parsley.

Eight treasure soup

serves **4–6**
preparation time **15–20 minutes**
cooking time **about 15 minutes**

5 cups Chicken Stock (see page 9)
   or water
$^1/_3$ cup frozen peas
$^1/_3$ cup frozen corn
1 small boneless, skinless chicken
   breast, about $^1/_4$ lb, cut into very
   thin strips
1 cup fresh shiitake mushrooms,
   stalks removed, very thinly sliced
3 tablespoons soy sauce,
   or to taste
2 tablespoons rice wine or
   dry sherry
1 tablespoon cornstarch
$^1/_2$ cup cooked peeled shrimp,
   defrosted and dried thoroughly
   if frozen
3–4 thin slices cooked ham, sliced
$^2/_3$ cup firm tofu, drained and
   thinly sliced
$^1/_2$ cup fresh baby spinach leaves,
   very finely shredded
salt and pepper

1 Bring the stock or water to a boil in a large pot. Add the frozen peas and corn, and simmer for 3 minutes. Add the chicken, mushrooms, soy sauce, and rice wine or sherry. Stir well and simmer for 3 minutes.

2 Blend the cornstarch to a paste with a little cold water, then pour into the soup and stir to mix. Simmer, stirring, for 1–2 minutes, or until the soup thickens.

3 Lower the heat and add the shrimp, ham, tofu, and spinach. Simmer for about 2 minutes, or until the spinach is just wilted, stirring once or twice. Take care to stir gently so that the tofu does not break up. Taste and add salt and pepper if necessary, plus more soy sauce, if liked. Serve piping hot.

Wheat noodle soup with marinated chicken

serves **4–6**
preparation time **30 minutes**,
plus marinating
cooking time **20–25 minutes**

10 oz boneless, skinless chicken
   breasts
1 teaspoon turmeric
2 teaspoons salt
2 lemon grass stalks
3 tablespoons peanuts, skinned
   and roasted
3 tablespoons long-grain
   white rice
2 tablespoons vegetable oil
1 onion, chopped
3 garlic cloves, crushed
2 inch piece of fresh ginger root,
   peeled and finely chopped
$1/4$ teaspoon paprika
2 red bird's eye chilies, chopped
2–3 tablespoons Thai fish sauce
$3^3/4$ cups water
$1/2$ lb wheat noodles

To serve
3 hard-boiled eggs, halved
2 tablespoons chopped fresh
   cilantro leaves
3 scallions, finely chopped
Thai fish sauce
crushed dried chili
1–2 tablespoons balachaung
   (optional)

1 Cut the chicken breasts into 1 inch cubes. Mix the turmeric with the salt and rub it into the cubes of chicken. Cover and leave to stand for 30 minutes.

2 Bruise the lemon grass with the side of a rolling pin to release the flavor. Finely crush the roasted peanuts in a food processor or using a mortar and pestle. Heat a dry frying pan and toast the rice until golden brown, then finely crush it to a powder in a food processor or spice grinder.

3 Heat the oil in a large pot, add the onion, and cook until just softened. Add the dry marinated chicken together with the lemon grass, garlic, ginger, paprika, and chilies. Add the fish sauce and measured water, and bring to a boil.

4 Lower the heat and simmer gently. Mix the crushed peanuts and ground rice, and add to the pan. Simmer for 10–15 minutes, or until the chicken has cooked through and the broth thickened slightly.

5 Meanwhile, bring a pot of water to a boil, add the noodles, and cook for 3–4 minutes, or until just tender. Drain and refresh with cold water, then divide between large soup bowls.

6 Ladle the chicken soup over the noodles and serve topped with hard-boiled eggs, chopped cilantro, and scallions. Add an extra splash of fish sauce and a sprinkling of crushed dried chili and balachaung, if using, to taste. Eat the soup with a spoon and fork.

tip Balachaung is a hot Burmese condiment made from deep-fried shallots, garlic, chilies, and dried shrimp. You can just use deep-fried shallots, which, like balachaung, are available from Oriental stores.

Index

Acknowledgments

Executive Editor: Nicky Hill
Senior Editor: Rachel Lawrence
Executive Art Editor: Leigh Jones
Designer: Tony Truscott
Picture Researcher: Luzia Strohmayer
Production Controller: Manjit Sihra

Octopus Publishing Group Limited /Frank Adam 8, 110 /Stephen Conroy 100–101, 109 /David Loftus 93 /Jeremy Hopley 39 /David Jordan 73 /Sandra Lane 28, 54, 51–52, 57 /William Lingwood 21 /David Loftus 2, 22, 50, 69, 94, 97, 99, 118, 125 /Diana Miller 35, 66, 90, 107, 115 /Peter Myers 7, 11, 17, 62 /Sean Myers 32–33, 41, 83, 89 /William Reavell 24, 43, 45, 82, 85, 111, 113, 119 /Simon Smith 47, 59 /Ian Wallace 3, 4, 15, 25, 27, 31, 37, 60, 67, 71, 76, 78, 81, 87, 103, 106, 117, 123 /Philip Webb 1, 12–13, 19, 49, 65, 75, 105, 121.